THINGS to Make & Do FOR Pentecost

Also available in this series:
Things to Make and Do for Advent and Christmas
Things to Make and Do for Lent and Easter

One more book will soon be available
in the Things to Make and Do series:

Things to Make and Do Anytime

THINGS to Make & Do FOR Pentecost

Written and Compiled
by Martha Bettis Gee

BRIDGE
resources

Bridge Resources
Louisville, Kentucky

Book interior and cover design by Diane Bridgwater Cooke
Illustrations by Debora Weber

First Edition

Published by Bridge Resources
Louisville, Kentucky

Website address: http://www.bridgeresources.org

PRINTED IN THE UNITED STATES OF AMERICA
98 99 00 01 02 03 04 05 06 07 — 10 9 8 7 6 5 4 3 2 1

Library of Congress Cataloging-in-Publication Data
Gee, Martha Bettis, date.
    Things to make and do for Pentecost / written and compiled by Martha Bettis Gee. — 1st ed.
        p.   cm.
    Includes index.
    ISBN 1-57895-017-1
    1. Pentecost. 2. Bible crafts. 3. Christian education of children. 4. Christian education—Activity programs. 5. Creative activities and seat work.
    I. Title.
    BT121.2.G43   1998
    246—dc21   97-35299

Contents

Introduction

As the traditional school year draws to a close, children eagerly anticipate days of vacation. Even where year-round school is in place, it is a time of both endings and beginnings. There is a stirring of the spirit afoot—the spirit of longing for the endless days of summer. And that spirit stirs us whether we have a three-week or a three-month vacation.

The Day of Pentecost, the culmination of the Easter cycle in the church year, is the only Christian festival that has not been co-opted by our culture for commercial use. At Pentecost, something mysterious, powerful, and awe-inspiring took place that transformed a small, ragged group of disciples into a force that would change the world. On that day the church received the gift of the Holy Spirit, a gift that empowered Christians to witness to the resurrected Lord. It is a gift that at the same time draws us together from all races and cultures and times and sends us forth as the visible expression of the invisible power of God.

Through the ages the church has interpreted that powerful mystery with sensory images—tongues of flame, a descending dove, and a powerful wind. Each metaphor reveals a slightly different facet of the Holy Spirit, just as a dancing flame changes from moment to moment. That picture takes on even more tangible form as the Spirit is evidenced in the faces of the faithful—people from all cultures and walks of life. In the daily rhythms of the community of faith as it engages in ministry, the Spirit lives.

About This Book

The activities in this book have been gathered from many places. Some were a part of curriculum resources over many years. Some are the fruit of twelve years' teaching experience and twenty-five years of working with children. Some came from the creative minds of colleagues and friends who love children. And some came from children themselves. Like all good creative activities, each one began as an idea that took shape in the hands of those who used it.

At the heart of the creative process is the working of the Spirit, moving and shaping and transforming the person engaged in the act of creation. Every activity suggested here awaits the unique approach that only you and your group of children can bring to it.

Using Creative Activities with Children

● ●

Creative activities . . .

- provide an avenue for God's Spirit to speak to children
- give children a vehicle for expressing ideas, concepts, and feelings
- express each person's uniqueness as a child of God, a creation unlike any other
- speak to the variety of gifts of the Spirit within the community of faith

Guidelines for Using These Activities

- Allow plenty of time for exploration and expression. Creative activities cannot be rushed!
- Give enough directions for children to create, but allow for variations and alternative uses of materials.
- Model good stewardship for children by being intentional about a wise use of resources. Many activities in this book use found materials or scraps left over from previous activities. Help children to understand that when they find creative uses for scraps of construction paper, they are being good stewards of our world. In the same way, help children to learn to take good care of art materials. Securely closing the tops of glue bottles or tempera-paint containers and carefully putting away scissors and crayons ensures that these expensive art materials last as long as possible.
- Recognizing that every night one-fourth of the world's children go hungry, we do not recommend the use of food in art activities. One exception is the use of modeling dough and play dough made from flour and salt. We have not yet found a satisfactory substitute for these materials.

Young children can understand Pentecost in these terms.

- Pentecost is the birthday of the church.
- We can celebrate the church's birthday by singing, praying, and hearing stories from the Bible and about the church and how it grew.
- Red is a happy color that reminds us of the church's birthday.
- The church is people who love God.
- I am an important part of my church.

Younger elementary children build on these understandings.

- At Pentecost the church received the gift of the Holy Spirit.
- The dove, the flame, and the wind remind us of God's Holy Spirit.
- The church is made up of all kinds of people from all times and places who love God.
- The church prays, worships God, cares for others, and shares with those in need.

Older elementary children add deeper understandings.

- While we cannot fully understand the Holy Spirit, we can see evidence of the work of the Spirit in the life of the church and in its work in the world.
- Symbols for the Spirit, like the dove, the flame, and the wind, all help us express some facet of the nature of the Spirit.

Day of Pentecost

Then afterward . . .
   I will pour out my Spirit on all flesh;
your sons and your daughters shall prophesy,
   your old shall dream dreams,
   and your young shall see visions.

(Joel 2:28)

On the Day of Pentecost, God's Spirit poured forth on the gathered disciples.

On Pentecost, we experience the Spirit
- as a cleansing, troubling wind stirring us to the core of our being
- as tongues of fire forging our will and refining our purpose
- as the descending dove of presence, calling us into community and sending that community forth to serve

On Pentecost, we celebrate the gift of the Spirit
- in our common life together
- in our diversity of culture and language and custom
- in the variety of our gifts and expressions of call

Wind

In Acts, we read that the people who gathered for the feast of Pentecost heard a noise that sounded like the rushing of a strong wind. The wind reminds us that the Holy Spirit, while unseen, exhibits power evident in the life of the church.

Wind Socks

● ● ● ● ● ● ● ● ● ● ● ● ● ● ●

Crepe-Paper Wind Socks

Young Children and Younger Elementary Children

What You Need

- Poster-board strips about 2" x 18"
- Red and white crepe-paper streamers
- Stapler or tape
- Scissors
- String
- Hole punch

What You Do

1. Show children how to cut crepe-paper streamers two to three feet long. They then tape or staple the streamers to one side of a poster-board strip, stopping about an inch from one end.

2. When the streamers are attached, children can overlap the ends of the poster-board strip and tape together.

3. Using a hole punch, make four holes equidistant from each other on the cardboard ring. Children can tie eighteen-inch pieces of string through the holes, pull the four strings up, and knot them together to join them about twelve inches above the ring. Attach a longer piece of string to the three (see below).

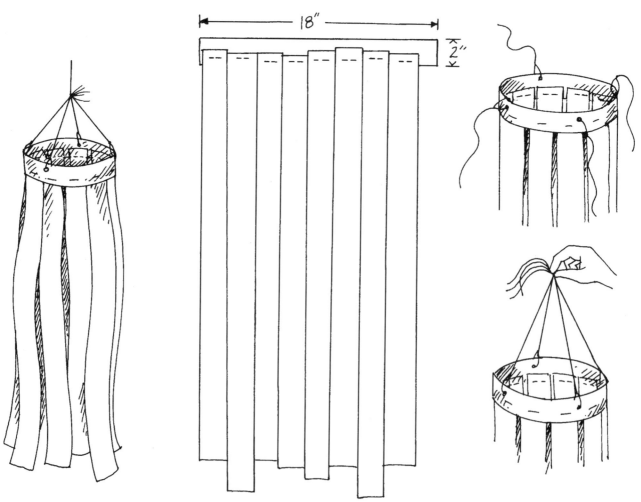

Tissue-Paper Wind Socks

Older Elementary Children

What You Need

- Poster-board strips, about 2" x 18"
- Red, yellow, and orange tissue paper
- Stapler or tape
- Scissors
- String
- Hole punch

What You Do

1. Give each of the children a poster-board strip. Tell them to tape the strip together to make a ring, overlapping slightly.

2. Give each child three sheets of tissue paper, either all of one color or one sheet of each of the three colors. Tell them to tape the sides together.

3. Children then pull the corner of the tissue paper over the ring and tape in place. They work their way around the ring, pulling about an inch of the top of the tissue paper over the ring and taping it all the way around the ring. It may be easier to make one-inch cuts in the paper so it will fit more smoothly.

4. The tissue paper will overlap at the end, and children can either cut it off or continue going around the ring and taping it.

5. Using a hole punch, children can make four holes equidistant from each other on the cardboard ring. Children can tie eighteen-inch pieces of string through the holes, pull the four strings up, and knot them together to join them about twelve inches above the ring. Attach a longer piece of string to the three (see illustration below).

6. Show children how to cut the tissue paper into streamers. Starting at the bottom, ask them to cut the paper into strips an inch or two wide. They should not cut all the way to the top.

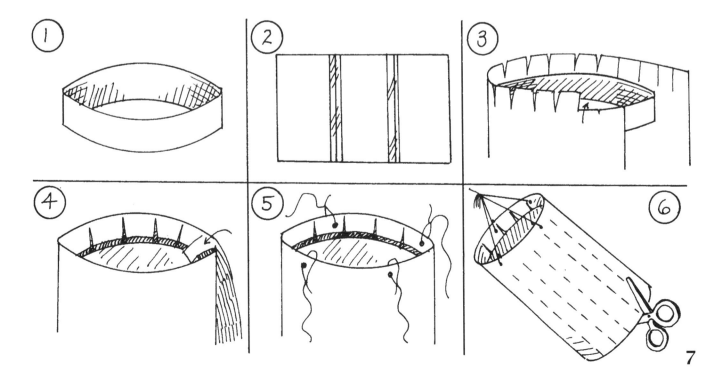

Mini Wind Socks

Children of All Ages

What You Need

- Cardboard tubes (bathroom tissue and paper-towel tubes)
- Birthday gift wrap
- Scissors
- Glue
- Self-curling ribbon
- Hole punch

What You Do

1. Tell the children that Pentecost is the birthday of the church and that they are going to use birthday wrapping paper to make a special, small wind sock.

2. Give each child a cardboard tube. Let him or her choose some birthday wrapping paper, cut it to fit the tube, and tape it on. Younger children may need help in cutting the paper to fit.

3. Let each child use a hole punch to make three or four holes around the bottom of the tube. They should cut one or two long pieces of ribbon to tie in each hole, then curl the ends with scissors.

4. Show children how to punch two holes in the top of the tube equidistant from each other, tie ribbon in each hole, and then tie the two pieces together about three inches above the top. Attach another ribbon to the knot.

5. Hang all the wind socks outside from a low tree branch for everyone to enjoy before the children take them home.

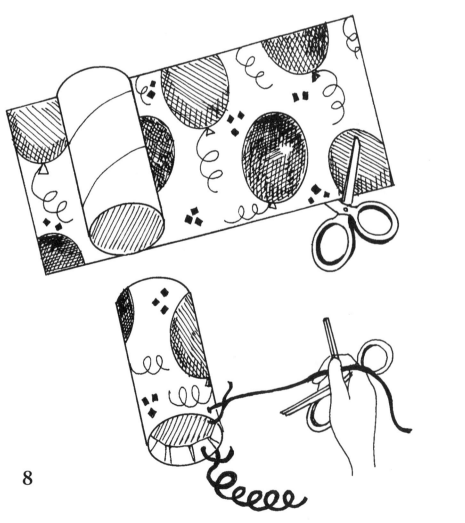

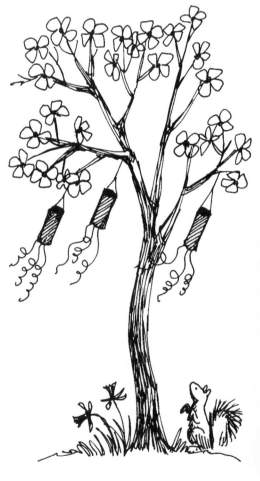

8

Easiest-Ever Wind Socks

Young Children

Here is a very simple wind sock for the youngest children.

What You Need

- White construction paper
- Red felt-tipped markers
- Red crepe-paper streamers
- Stapler
- Red yarn

What You Do

1. Give each child a sheet of white construction paper and a red marker. Suggest to the children that they draw a picture with the marker, perhaps a happy birthday picture for the church.

2. Help each child to staple crepe-paper streamers about eight inches long to the bottom edge of the paper, then staple the paper together to form a cylinder.

3. Staple two pieces of red yarn to the top of the cylinder, tie them together about six to eight inches above the top, and add another longer piece to hold the wind sock.

♣ And More . . .

Older children can copy the Pentecost passage from Acts 2:1–13 on the sheets of paper using felt-tipped red markers. They can then complete the wind sock according to the directions.

9

Kites
● ● ● ● ● ● ● ● ● ●
Circular Kites

Older Elementary Children

These small kites can be made entirely by older children. Younger children might enjoy drawing on circular pieces of white paper with red markers, then gluing their pictures on a completed kite.

What You Need

- 1 1/2-inch ring cut from a 42-ounce oatmeal box (you can get several from each box), or poster board cut 1/2" x 19"
- Poster-board template for circle measuring 8 1/2 inches in diameter
- Red crepe paper
- Rubber bands
- Stapler
- White crepe-paper streamers
- Hole punch
- Ball of kite string for each kite

What You Do

1. Let each child use the poster-board circle pattern to trace and cut a circle from the red crepe paper.

2. Show children how to lay the crepe-paper circle over the cardboard ring and even it out, then put one staple in the ring to secure the paper. Children then go half way around the ring and put in a second staple. Holding the paper and turning the ring, they should put in six more staples at evenly spaced intervals around the ring.

3. Using the hole punch, children should then put two holes in the ring equidistant from each other.

4. Children can stretch a rubber band around the ring to smooth out the crepe paper.

5. Tell children to cut a twelve-inch piece of string and to tie one end in each of the two holes. They can attach the ball of string to the center of this piece.

6. Children can staple on white crepe-paper streamers to make a tail.

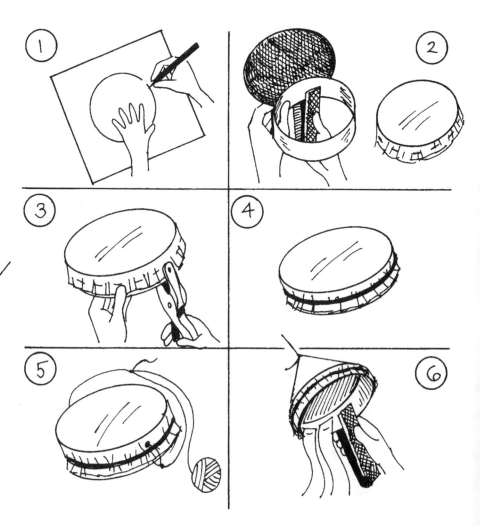

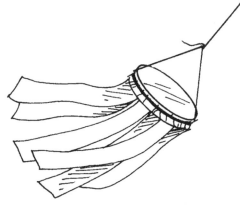

Shower Curtain Kite

Older Elementary Children

What You Need

- Sheets of newspaper at least 36" x 40"
- Three dowel sticks per kite, 3/8" x 36"
- White shower curtain liners (one for every four kites)
- One roll of cloth sticky tape (minimum 80 inches per roll) per kite
- One ball of kite string
- Permanent felt marker
- Hole punch

What You Do

1. In advance, cut a newspaper pattern using the dimensions below. Tape the shower curtain to a table, and have a child help you outline the kite pattern with a permanent marker on the plastic.

2. Talk with the children about messages and symbols of Pentecost that they might use to decorate their kites. Let them use red markers to draw doves or flames or to print words such as, "Come, Holy Spirit." They can then cut out the kite shapes.

3. Show children how to cut seven ten-inch strips and one six-inch strip from the roll of cloth sticky tape. Have them lay the strips sticky side up and place a dowel lengthwise in the center of each strip. Show them how to press down on the dowel so that it adheres, then lay the dowel and tape carefully in place on the kite materials, pressing tape on either side of dowel.

4. Have children cut two one-and-a-half inch squares of tape and apply to the points where the bridle of the kite will be attached (see below). Punch holes for string.

5. Give each child eighty inches of string. They can tie one end through each of the holes in the kite.

6. Attach thirty inches of string to the bottom of the kite for a tail loop.

7. Children can tie a flying line to the midpoint of the bridle line. Now the kite is ready to fly. If they find a tail is needed, they can use strips of red cloth to make one.

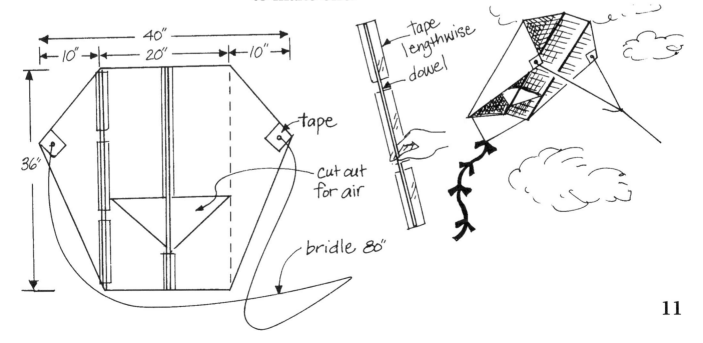

40"

10" → ← 20" → ← 10"

36"

tape

cut out for air

bridle 80"

tape lengthwise dowel

Whirligigs, Mobiles, and Wind Devices

● ● ● ● ● ● ● ● ● ● ●

Pentecost Pinwheel

Young Children and Younger Elementary Children

What You Need

- Red or white paper, about eight-inch square
- Scissors
- Straight pins
- Unsharpened pencils with erasers

What You Do

1. In advance, draw diagonal intersecting lines on the paper (see below). Younger elementary children may be able to do this themselves. Have children cut on the lines to within one quarter inch of the point of intersection.

2. Following the diagram on this page, have children fold up the paper to the center. They then put a straight pin through all four corners into the eraser of the pencil.

♣ And More . . .

Before making the pinwheels, children could use the blow-painting technique to embellish white paper. Use a medicine dropper to put a small amount of red paint in the center of the square of paper. Then let the children use soda straws to blow the paint around on the paper to make a design. Let the paper squares dry thoroughly before the children make the pinwheels.

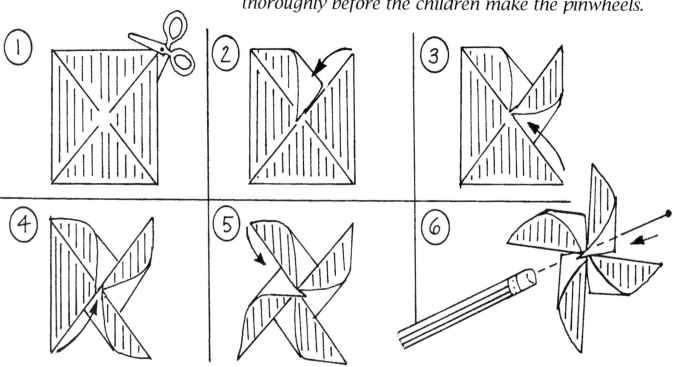

Whirligigs

Older Elementary Children

What You Need

- Templates from dove body pattern (see p. 78)
- White poster board
- White computer or typing paper, about 6 inches square
- Instructions for making pinwheels (see p. 12)
- Unsharpened pencils with erasers (2 per whirligig)
- White plastic tape
- Straight pins
- Pencils
- Black fine-lined, felt-tipped markers
- Scissors
- Craft sticks
- Small flat cans (such as for cat food or tuna)
- Paintbrushes and red enamel paint
- Modeling clay (plaster of paris can also be used)

What You Do

1. In advance, have children paint the cans red using enamel paint and set aside to dry thoroughly.

2. Have the children cut a dove body from the white poster board (dove pattern, p. 78). Children then cut a small slit in the dove body.

3. Show the children how to tape together two unsharpened pencils so that the erasers are at either end.

4. Tell children to put a ball of modeling clay in the can. Children then tape a craft stick to the dove body and insert it in the clay.

5. Show children how to slide the taped pencils through the slit in the dove's body until there is an equal length on both sides.

6. Children then make two pinwheels according to the directions on p. 12 and attach them to the erasers of the pencils with straight pins.

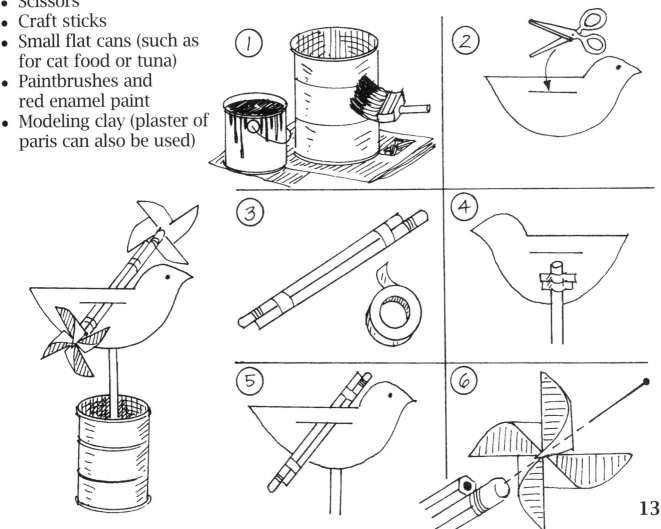

13

Pentecost Wind Chime

Young Children and Younger Elementary Children

What You Need

- Red plastic coat hanger
- Red ribbon or yarn
- Scissors
- Clear tape
- Variety of found objects that would make a sound when they make contact with each other (e.g., old metal knife, fork, or spoon; nails or screws of various sizes; large metal paper clips)

What You Do

1. Have the children cut yarn or ribbon into pieces of various lengths and tie one end of each piece to an object. Tie the other end to the hanger.

2. Slide the yarn back and forth until the mobile is balanced.

3. Wrap clear tape around the yarn or ribbon at the hanger end to secure it in place and to keep it from sliding.

4. Use a piece of yarn or ribbon to hang the wind chime.

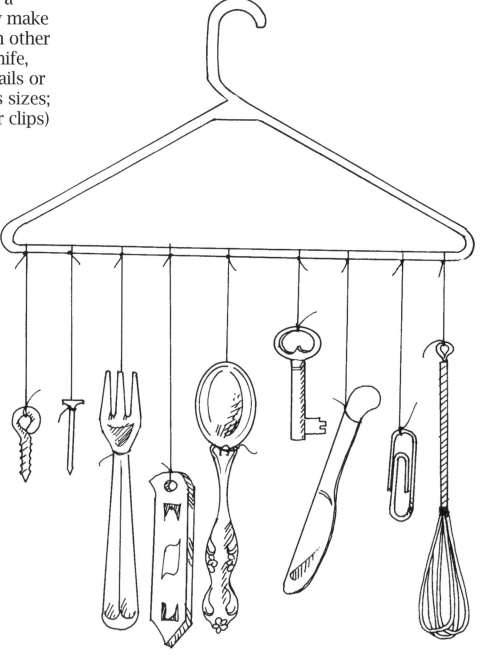

A Mobile Banner

Older Elementary Children

Because the coming of the Holy Spirit at Pentecost is so often represented by two dynamic concrete symbols (the dove and the flame), and by the wind that is recognized only by its effects, a mobile banner is particularly appropriate for the season.

Making a mobile requires some patience in order to achieve balance. Older elementary children will need the help of youth or adults.

What You Need

- Coat hanger
- Monofilament fishing line
- White and red poster board
- Cardboard templates of dove and flame (see pp. 79 and 80)
- Fine-lined black and red markers
- Pencils
- White glue
- Newsprint and markers
- Tape
- Scissors
- Hole punch

What You Do

1. Talk with children about what words they might like to put on their banners. List their suggestions on the newsprint. Some possibilities are, "Come, Holy Spirit," "We Are One in the Spirit," or perhaps the words of *Acts 2:1-4.*

2. Tell children to cut two doves from the white poster board. They will also need to cut several flames from the red poster board, depending on how many words they want on their banner.

3. Tell the children to use their pencils to lightly print the words on the banner pieces, then use black or red markers to go over the pencil lines. They should print the same words on the two dove pieces and use the front and back of the flame pieces.

4. Show children how to attach one dove piece to the hanger by taping it on the back. They can then use white glue to attach the second dove.

5. Attach the flames to the banner by punching holes in the tops, tying on monofilament of various lengths, and then tying the monofilament to the dove.

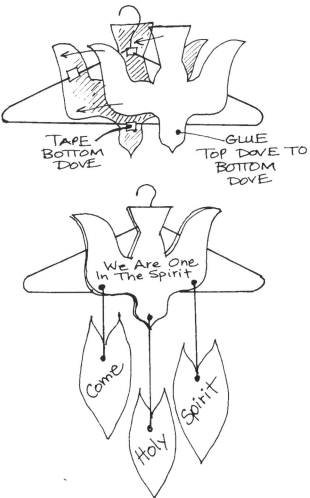

TAPE BOTTOM DOVE

GLUE TOP DOVE TO BOTTOM DOVE

We Are One In The Spirit

Come   Holy   Spirit

15

Embroidery Hoop Mobile

Older Elementary Children

What You Need

- 14-inch wood or plastic embroidery hoop
- Pencils
- Red and white crepe-paper
- Red crepe-paper streamers
- Scissors
- Tape
- Glue
- Strong thread, about 18 inches
- Dove pattern (see p. 79)

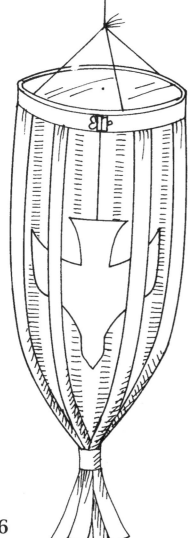

What You Do

1. Have the children open the embroidery hoop and place the solid hoop on a length of red crepe paper. Tell them to trace around the hoop lightly with a pencil.

2. Tell them to cut about three-quarter inch outside the pencil line.

3. Show the children how to cut varying lengths of streamers from four feet to six feet long, and tape them all the way around the crepe-paper circle.

4. Have them place the crepe-paper circle on top of the bottom half of the hoop, with the streamers fanning out. They then put the top half over the circle, stretch the paper to fit, and close the two halves.

5. Show the children how to make the crepe-paper dove. They cut two doves from white crepe paper using the pattern on p. 79. Then they glue the two dove shapes together on three sides, stuff lightly with tissue paper, and glue the fourth side closed. Have the children cut two wings using the pattern, stretching the paper edges slightly to flare, and glue to the body.

6. From the exact center of the crepe-paper covered hoop, suspend a strong thread about eighteen inches long. Thread the other end through the dove's body, and tie a knot to secure.

7. Bring the red crepe-paper streamers together just under the suspended dove. Secure with a short piece of crepe paper (see illustration).

8. To hang, thread three strong threads equidistant around the edges of the embroidery hoop. Tie together about twelve inches above the hoop; then balance and hang.

♣ And More . . .

—Although red and white are the traditional colors of Pentecost, children might want to add orange and yellow streamers to their mobiles.

—Suspend from the hoop poster-board flames with phrases such as "Come, Holy Spirit."

Things To Do

•••••••••••

A Guided Meditation on Wind and Flame

Younger and Older Elementary Children (or intergenerational groups)

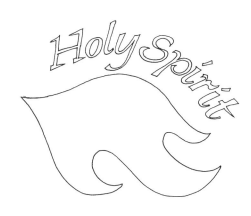

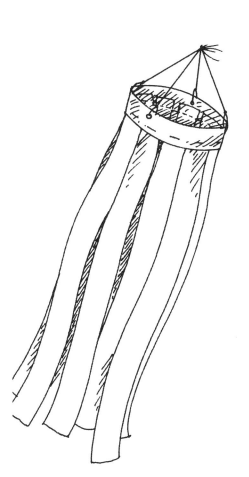

What You Do

1. Ask participants to find a comfortable place to sit. Say the following:

Before Jesus was born, the Jewish people had a festival called the Festival of Weeks. It commemorated the harvesting of the first foods grown in the spring. After Jesus' death and resurrection, Christians received the gift of the Holy Spirit during that festival. Now we celebrate that gift of the Holy Spirit to the church at Pentecost. The early Christians thought of God's Holy Spirit in two dramatic ways—the brilliant light of flames and a mighty wind.

2. Use the following guided meditation:

What is the Holy Spirit like?

Maybe the Holy Spirit is like the wind. Have you ever seen the wind? No—but you have felt the wind on your skin and have seen what the wind can do as it moves the tops of trees and pushes waves in to shore.

Maybe the Holy Spirit is like fire. A fire gives us warmth, comfort, and light.

Come away for a moment to an imaginary campsite. There we'll meet the Holy Spirit of God.

(Read slowly)

Shut your eyes and relax. (*Pause*) Take a deep breath and let the Spirit of God enter your body. Breathe deeply. (*Pause*) Feel your body relax and welcome God's Spirit.

You are in a campground and it is quiet and peaceful. Breathe deeply. Smell the pine needles. (*Pause)* Smell the smoke from the campfire. (*Pause*) Smell the damp earth.

Invite the Holy Spirit to come to you. The Spirit will come as wind. Feel a strong breeze in your face. It is refreshing and exciting. (*Pause*) Listen to the wind in the pine trees. (*Pause*) Hear the wind rustling the leaves by your tent. (*Pause*) Come, Holy Spirit. (*Pause*) The wind is strong enough to fly a kite. You have a beautiful kite—red, blue, yellow, with a long swirling tail. (*With excitement*) Run to the open field.

Let your kite soar behind you. Feel the wind in your face as you look up. Your kite rolls and dips in the wind. (*Pause*)

Invite the Holy Spirit to come to you. The Spirit will come as fire. It is night and the campsite is quiet. Curl up in front of your campfire. (*Pause*) You stare into the flames. Sometimes the fire glows softly. Sometimes the flames dance and snap. (*Pause*) Come, Holy Spirit. (*Pause*) The night is chilly, but the fire wraps you in warmth and comfort. (*Pause*) Look around. It is dark beyond your campsite. You are a little frightened to walk off in the dark, but within the circle of warmth and light from your fire, you have courage. (*Pause*)

Now . . . open your eyes. Breathe slowly.

Sometimes the Holy Spirit comes with joy and dancing like your kite soaring in the wind. Sometimes it comes like a quiet, glowing ember. Thanks be to God.

Wind Play

Younger and Older Elementary Children

The wind blows where it chooses, and you hear the sound of it, but you do not know where it comes from or where it goes. But it is with everyone who is born of the Spirit.

(*John 3:8*)

What You Need

- Electric fan
- Scrap paper
- Strips of paper, 8" x 1"
- Broomstick
- Tape
- Two heavy books
- Index card
- Glass soda bottle
- Candle in holder and matches
- Sheets of copy paper (for making paper airplanes)
- Bible

What You Do

1. Read the account of Pentecost from *Acts 2* and the passage from John on the left. Tell the children that we often compare the Holy Spirit to the wind because we cannot see the Spirit, but we are aware of the working of the Spirit in our lives.

2. Have the children tear the scrap paper into small bits and put them on a tabletop. Hold a fan over the paper. Tell the children to watch to see in which direction the bits will be blown if the fan is pointed toward them. What happens to the pieces of paper that are on the edge of the moving air?

3. Does the wind blow in the same direction at ground level as it does three or six feet higher? To find out, have the children tape the paper strips onto a broomstick in several places, so they stick out like flags. Take the broom outside into the wind and let children take turns holding it at different levels. Do the strips of paper move in the same way at ground level as at six feet above the ground?

4. Have the children place two books that are exactly the same size on the table about three inches apart. Lay a card across the gap. Let the children try to blow the card off the books. After several have tried with no success, explain that when you blow under the card, between the books, the fast-moving air causes a reduced pressure. The higher pressure above the card then pushes down and makes it cling to the books. When you blow down on the card, the air also pushes the card against the books. So, whether you blow over or under the card, it tends to cling to the books!

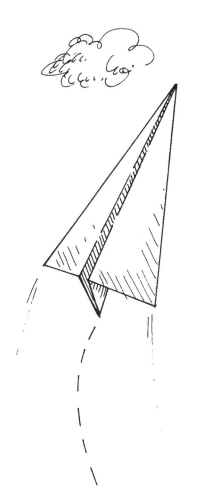

5. Place a glass soda bottle upright on the table. Put a lighted candle right behind the bottle. Invite a child to blow out the candle from in front of the bottle. Now place a book upright on the table. Let another child try to blow out the candle in back of the book.

6. Let each child fold a paper airplane, throw it, and watch it glide. Now tell the children to turn the back ends up slightly on their airplanes and fly them again. If the ends are bent too sharply, the airplane may stall in midair and fall. Let children try to make their airplanes move fast enough to make a complete loop in the air. Now have them turn the back ends down slightly. Then try bending one side up and the other down. Each of these little changes makes a big difference in the way the airplane flies because of the way it moves in the wind.

Bubble Blowing

Children of All Ages

What You Need

- Bubble-blowing solution
- Shallow, flat pan
- Red food coloring (optional)
- Pipe cleaners

What You Do

1. Let the children use the pipe cleaners to make bubble blowers. They can make a circle with one pipe cleaner, or twist two or three together. Circles, ovals, triangles, and squares all make interesting bubbles.

2. Pour the bubble solution into the flat pan and add red food coloring.

Note: This activity is the most fun outside on a breezy day. If you are doing it inside, do not add red food coloring to the bubble solution.

3. Have children dip their pipe-cleaner bubble blowers into the bubble solution and experiment with blowing bubbles.

Doves

At Jesus' baptism, so the Gospel writers tell us, the Holy Spirit descended on him in the form of a dove.

Flying Dove

Younger and Older Elementary Children

What You Need

- White typing or computer printer paper
- Scissors
- Pencils
- Pattern on this page
- Clear tape
- Black fine-lined, felt-tipped markers

What You Do

1. Trace or photocopy the pattern on this page to make templates for the children.

2. Show children how to trace the dove template on white paper, cut it out, and fold it as shown on the pattern.

3. Have them use clear tape to tape the halves shut at the nose and shoulders.

4. Children can use fine-lined black markers to draw on eyes.

5. Children can fly the doves like paper airplanes.

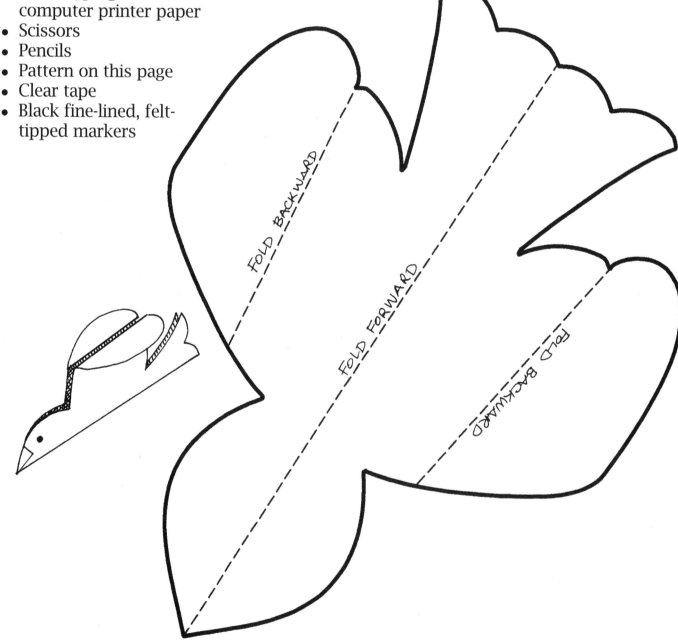

FOLD BACKWARD

FOLD FORWARD

FOLD BACKWARD

Curly Dove

Younger Elementary Children

This is an easy way to make dove ornaments to hang on a mobile.

What You Need

- White construction-paper strips, 1/2" x 12"
- Pencils
- Stapler
- Thread

What You Do

1. Children can staple together two or three strips of paper about two inches in from each end to make the bird's body. Show them how to stagger the ends of the strips so that one strip forms the curve of the body.

2. Show children how to curl the ends of the construction-paper strips by rolling them up on a pencil.

3. Hang by running a thread through the dove's body.

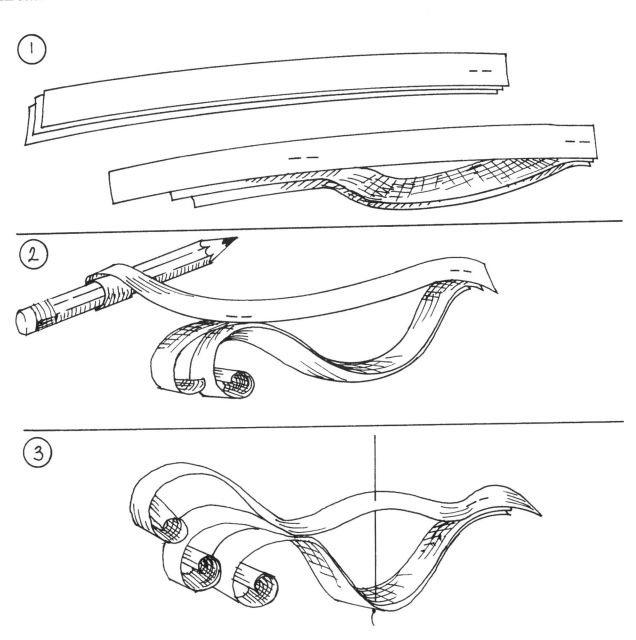

Quilled Dove

Older Elementary Children

This technique, although not complicated, is time-consuming. The intricate detailing on the finished dove gives the paper depth and texture.

What You Need

- White typing or computer printing paper, cut into strips about 1/2 inch wide
- Pattern for dove's body and wings (p. 78)
- Scissors
- Round toothpicks
- Straight pins
- Waxed paper
- White glue
- Red poster board (one sheet for every four children)

What You Do

1. Demonstrate for the children how to make some of the basic quilling shapes on this page. Explain that they can coil the paper around a round toothpick and tear off the strip when the shape is complete. They can dab a bit of white glue on the end of the strip to secure it.

2. Show the children how to cover a small portion of the dove's body with white glue, then attach the quilled shapes to the glue.

3. When the dove's body is covered and the glue is dry, mount the dove on a piece of red poster board.

Quilling Shapes

Basic Rolls:

Loose   Raindrop

Tight   Feather

Eye   Square

Triangle

Pressed Heart

Scrolls:

Scroll   "V"

"S" Shape   Modified Heart

Open Heart   Decorative Scroll

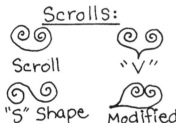

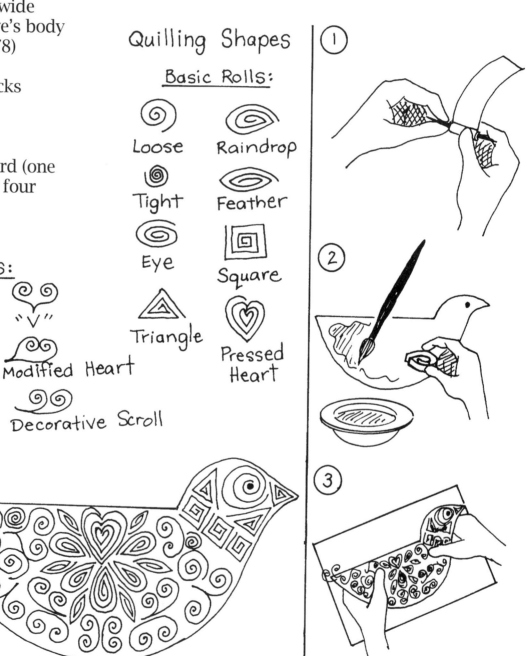

Winged Dove

Young Children

This is an easy dove for children to make as soon as they are able to make simple fans.

What You Need

- White poster board
- White typing or computer printer paper
- Dove pattern (p. 78)
- Fine-lined black markers

What You Do

1. In advance, use the pattern on p. 78 to cut the dove's body. Make a slit for the dove's wing.

2. Show children how to accordion pleat the typing paper to make the dove's wings. Then slide the wings through the slit in the body.

3. Children can use markers to add eyes.

25

Handprint Dove

Younger Elementary Children

What You Need

- Heavy white paper
- Pencils
- Scissors
- Black fine-lined, felt-tipped markers
- 8 ¹/₂" x 11" red construction paper

What You Do

1. Have the children trace their hands with their thumbs stretched out and their fingers together.

2. Children can then cut out the outline of their hand and glue to red construction paper.

3. Have the children use black markers to make an eye and a beak.

♣ And More . . .

Children can combine cutout handprint doves with printed handprint flames (see p. 30) to make a Pentecost banner or picture.

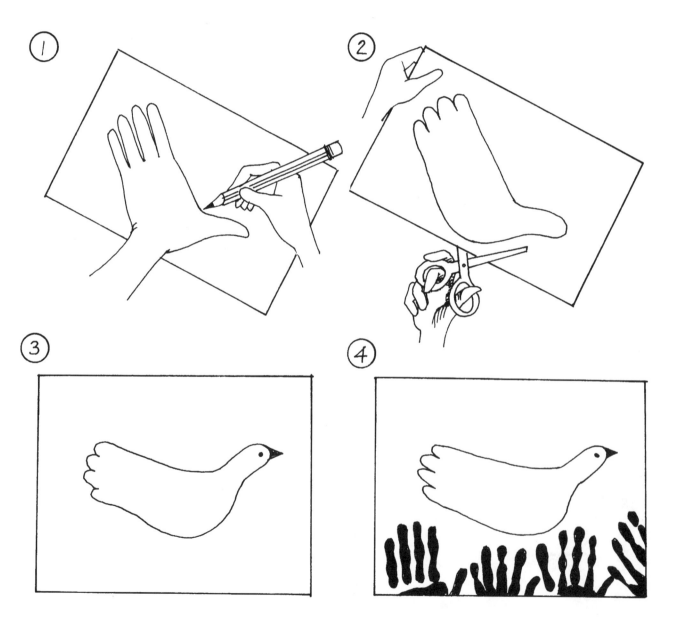

26

Flames and Fire

• • • • • • • • • • • •

The Acts account of the Pentecost event tells us that divided tongues like fire seemed to rest over each person. Flames and fire remind us of God's gift of the Holy Spirit at Pentecost and of the power that energized the early church as a result.

Showering Fire Petals

Younger Elementary Children

In some European countries a custom is observed on Pentecost Sunday. Through a hole in the ceiling, red flowers and petals of flowers are showered on the congregation below. This symbolizes the experience of fire that the disciples of Jesus knew at the coming of God's Spirit at Pentecost.

What You Need

- Red tissue paper
- Medium-sized brown paper lunch sacks
- Red construction paper
- Scissors
- Glue

What You Do

1. Tell the children about the European custom of showering the congregation with fire petals (see description on the left).

2. Let each child cut out construction-paper flames and glue them on a paper bag (see pattern on p. 80).

3. Tell children to cut the red tissue paper into flame or petal shapes. If they like, they can just cut the tissue into small bits rather than trying to make each piece resemble a flame. They should fill the bottom of the paper bag.

4. Children can process down the aisles during a Pentecost service, showering the congregation with petals of fire.

(Note: Both teachers and children will be more popular with the church staff if they volunteer to pick up the tissue-paper petals after the service!)

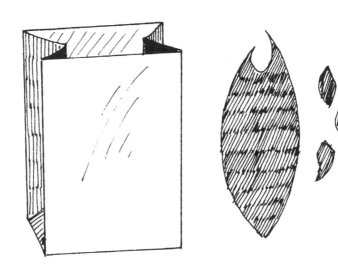

Tongues of Fire Tree

Younger and Older Elementary Children

What You Need

- Bare tree branch
- Coffee can
- Plaster of paris, pan, water, and mixing utensils
- Red, yellow, and orange curling ribbon
- Scissors

What You Do

1. Prepare plaster of paris according to package instructions, and pour into coffee can, filling about halfway. Allow to partially set. Insert tree branch into plaster, and carefully fill the can until it is about three-quarters full. Hold the branch steady until the plaster is set.

2. Ask the children what they suppose are the reasons artists created the kinds of symbols they did for the Holy Spirit. Assure them that the coming of the Holy Spirit is a mystery to everyone. The Spirit is God acting in our lives here and now. We know and feel the Holy Spirit's presence; the power of God is in and around us.

3. Tell the children that the ribbon looks like the flames that represent the Spirit. Let them cut ribbon in various lengths, curl it with scissors, and tie one end of each piece to the tree branch. Explain that the Tongues of Fire Tree will be their own symbol or reminder of the Pentecost story. Talk about what happened on Pentecost. The children might add other decorations, such as short sentences from Peter's speeches. Write these in English or in other languages that members of the group know how to write.

♣ **And More . . .**

Cut paper flames from red, orange, and yellow construction paper. Children can print the words "Come Holy Spirit" in various languages on the flames and use the ribbon to attach them to the tree branch.

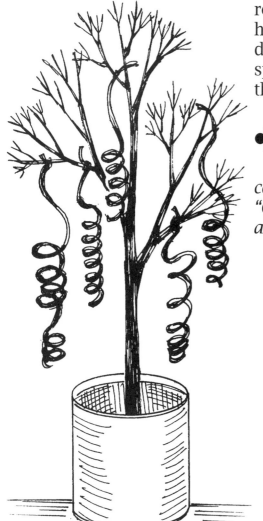

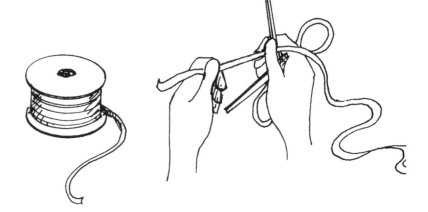

Fire Sticks

Younger Elementary Children

What You Need

- Red, orange, and yellow tissue paper
- Cardboard paper-towel rolls
- Mixture of white glue and water
- Paintbrushes
- Scissors

What You Do

1. Have children put two or three sheets of tissue paper together. Fire sticks look best with at least two colors of paper.

2. Show children how to paint the cardboard tube with the glue and water mix, gluing the first sheet of tissue paper to it and wrapping it around. (There will be extra tissue paper hanging down below the tube.) When the sheet begins to overlap, children can dab on a little more of the glue mixture so the sheet continues to adhere to the tube. When one sheet is glued on, children can glue on the second sheet the same way.

3. Set aside to dry.

4. When the glue is dry, children can cut the paper hanging free into strips about one inch wide, cutting almost up to the bottom of the tube.

5. Fire sticks can be waved in a Pentecost procession or parade.

29

Handprint Flames

Younger Elementary Children

The old standby of handprint painting can make an effective banner of flames!

What You Need

- Red, yellow, and orange tempera paint, mixed with a little liquid dishwashing detergent
- Large sheet of paper
- Pan of warm water and paper towels for cleanup

What You Do

1. Read *Acts 2:1-4.* Tell the children that flames are often used as a symbol of the Holy Spirit.

2. Let each child put his or her hand in one of the three colors of tempera paint. Children can then print their handprint on the paper. Encourage children to slightly overlap their handprints to more closely resemble flames. Children can wash off excess paint in the pan of water, then do a more thorough cleanup at a sink.

3. When the paint is dry, print "Come, Holy Spirit!" at the top of the paper and display.

Flame Sun Catchers

Older Elementary Children

These sun catchers can be used to make a Pentecost mobile or can be hung from a Pentecost tree. After Pentecost children can take them home to hang in a sunny window as a reminder of God's gift of the Holy Spirit.

What You Need

- Red, yellow, and orange plastic beads (10 for each sun catcher)
- 1 package clear plastic beverage cups
- Cookie sheets covered with aluminum foil
- Toothpick
- Oven (set on low temperature)
- String or thread

What You Do

1. Give each child a plastic cup. Tell the children to put ten plastic beads in the cup. They could use only red beads, or add some yellow or orange beads.

2. Set the oven on low temperature. Have the children put their cups on the cookie sheet, five or six cups to a sheet. Be sure there is space between the cups.

3. Put the cookie sheets in the oven until the cups flatten out and melt along with the beads.

4. Remove from the oven and allow to cool slightly. Before the plastic hardens, use a toothpick to make a hole in the top of each sun catcher.

5. Have the children attach a piece of string or thread through the hole for hanging on a mobile or a Pentecost tree.

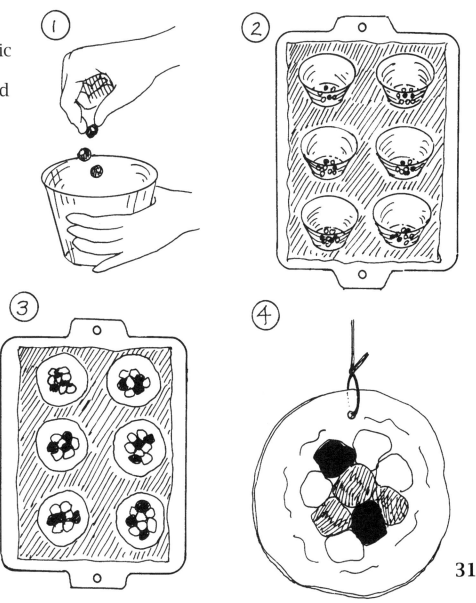

Tissue Lamination Flames

Younger and Older Elementary Children

What You Need

- Red, yellow, and orange tissue paper
- Flame pattern (see p. 80)
- Waxed paper
- Old newspapers
- Iron (set on lowest setting)
- Scissors
- Mixture of 1 part white glue to 2 parts water
- Brushes
- Red construction paper, 12" x 18"
- Black fine-lined, felt-tipped markers
- Pencils

What You Do

1. Cut two pieces of waxed paper about 8 ½" x 11" for each child. Tell the children to cut several flame shapes from tissue paper and arrange them in the center of one sheet of waxed paper. Show them how to paint over the shapes with the glue and water mixture.

2. Tell children to lay a second piece of waxed paper on top of the first. Sandwich between two or three thicknesses of newspaper, and let the children carefully iron over the paper until the waxed paper melts together. (Supervise carefully whenever children use an iron!)

3. Using the pattern on p. 80, cut a flame-shaped frame from the construction paper. Children can glue the waxed paper flame lamination to the back of the frame.

4. Children can use a pencil to lightly print *Acts 2:1-4* on the frame, then go over the pencil with a black fine-lined marker.

5. Display in a window.

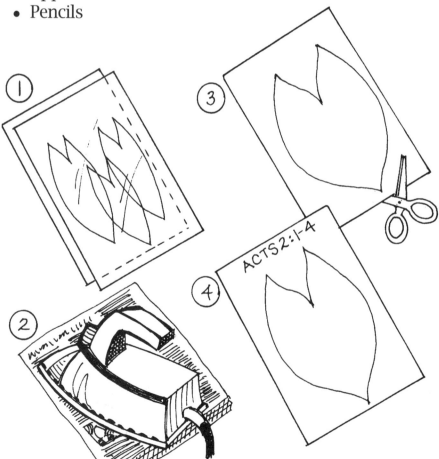

32

Happy Birthday, Church

●●●●●●●●●●●

In the early church, Christians celebrated from Easter until the fiftieth day after Easter, the *pentecoste*. Today we celebrate the gift of the Holy Spirit to that small group of believers. Children can understand Pentecost as the church's birthday, and for good reason. The infusion of the Holy Spirit into the community of faith did mark its birth.

A Birthday Gift for the Church

Younger and Older Elementary Children

In advance, check with your church pastor or governing body about what kinds of projects the children would have permission to do.

What You Need

- White drawing paper
- Colored felt-tipped markers
- Scrap materials (paper, rickrack and other trim, small buttons, and so forth)
- Newsprint
- White glue
- Glitter

What You Do

1. Read the *Acts 2:1-13,* the account of Pentecost, to the children. Then read *Acts 2:43-47.* Tell the children that Pentecost can be called the birthday of the church. Ask, What do you give to a church for its birthday? Ask children how they choose a gift for a friend. Suggest that perhaps that is also a good way to decide on a gift for the church. Tell children that one of the nicest gifts is to do something for the recipient.

2. Talk together about things the children could do to honor the church's birthday. List those things on newsprint. If children are having trouble thinking of gifts of service, you might get them started by suggesting that they offer to help in worship, using some of the poems, songs, prayers, and stories they have learned. Other suggestions are to have a birthday party for the church and invite the congregation, or plant flowers.

3. After you make your list, let the children choose a project, or you may want to choose two or three projects yourself and then let each child decide which one(s) they would like to do.

4. Invite the children to use the art supplies to make a birthday card for the church. They can decorate the outside of the card in any way they choose, using either the birthday theme or symbols of Pentecost. Inside, they should print what they will be giving the church for its birthday.

5. Deliver the cards to your pastor, educator, or a member of your church governing body.

33

A Birthday Party Game for the Church

Younger Elementary Children

This party game is like Pin the Tail on the Donkey.

What You Need

- White drawing paper
- Colored felt-tipped markers
- Scissors
- Stapler
- Mural or butcher paper with large church outline (see p. 82 for pattern, or make your own resembling your church building)
- Red construction-paper flames
- Straight pins
- Corkboard or bulletin board, or large piece of cardboard to back the church outline
- Blindfold

What You Do

1. In advance, mount the church outline on cardboard, or tack to bulletin board.

2. Ask each child to draw a picture on the white drawing paper of himself or herself. Encourage the children to make a drawing of their whole body.

3. Have them cut out their drawings and staple them to the church outline.

4. Play the game by choosing someone to be "it" and putting a blindfold on that child. Turn the child around three times and give him or her a construction-paper flame with a straight pin attached. The child then tries to attach the flame over the head of someone's picture.

5. Let everyone have a turn; then have a good time looking to see where the flames are pinned.

Happy Birthday Church Banner

Children of All Ages

What You Need

- One or two rolls of birthday wrapping paper (preferably patterned with balloons, birthday cakes, or other general depictions of celebration; do not choose paper with cartoon characters, etc.)
- Roll of butcher paper, shelf paper, or brown wrapping paper
- Colored felt-tipped markers
- Scissors
- Pencils
- Glue
- Sticks (optional)

What You Do

1. Invite each child to lie down on a length of butcher paper. Have a partner draw the outline of the child's head and shoulders with a pencil.

2. Tell the children to complete their body outlines by drawing facial features, hair, and clothing.

3. When finished, children can cut out the body outline.

4. Unroll the birthday wrapping paper. Children can glue their body outlines to this background. If you need more space, tape the second roll of paper to the first.

5. Display this banner in a hallway, or attach sticks to the sides so it can be carried in a procession. You can also add ribbons to the sides.

Flame Birthday Party Hats

Younger Elementary Children

What You Need

- White poster-board strips, 10" x 2"
- Red poster board
- Templates cut from flame pattern (see p. 80)
- Stapler
- Scissors
- Pencils
- Hole punch
- Red self-curling ribbon

What You Do

1. Let each child trace and cut out a large red flame. Show the children how to fold the flame along the dotted line indicated on the pattern. Staple the folded edge of the flame to the poster-board strip in two or three places. Fold up so that the flame stands up on the strip.

2. Let the children punch a hole in each end of the white strip. They can tie a piece of ribbon about eighteen inches long through each end of the strip.

3. Show children how to tie the ribbon under their chins to make a flame party hat.

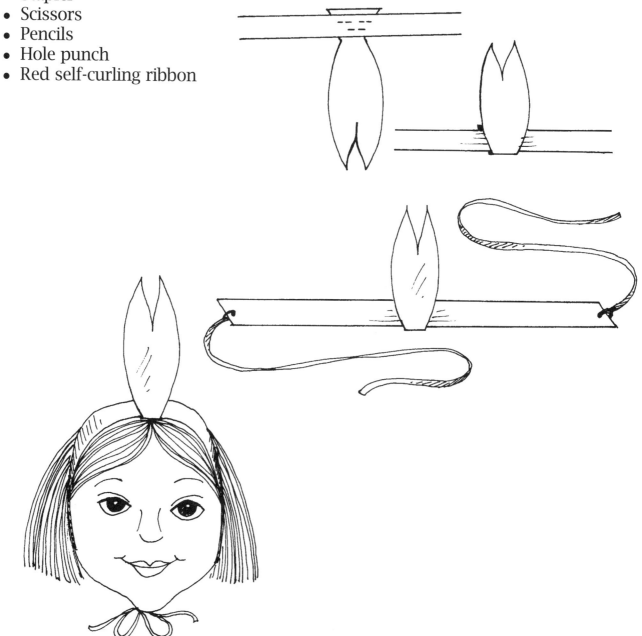

36

Make a Digeridoo

Younger Elementary Children

A digeridoo (DID-jer-I-DOO) is a long wind instrument from northern Australia. It is made from a hollowed-out tree trunk.

Did you ever hear of a
    digeridoo,
A digeridoo, a digeridoo,
Sing praises to God on a
    digeridoo,
The sound that you make
    will come back to you,
On a digeridoo, a digeridoo.

What You Need

- Long cardboard gift wrap tubes
- Birthday gift wrap paper with celebration design, such as balloons, party hats, and so forth (not cartoon characters or superheroes)
- White glue
- Red self-curling ribbon
- Scissors
- Hole punch

What You Do

1. Show the children how to cut a piece of birthday gift wrap and glue it to the cardboard tube.

2. When the glue is dry, children can punch two or three holes at one end of the tube and tie long pieces of self-curling ribbons to the tube, curling the ends of the ribbon.

3. To play the digeridoo, children cup their hands around the outside of the tube and blow sounds into the end that is not decorated with ribbons.

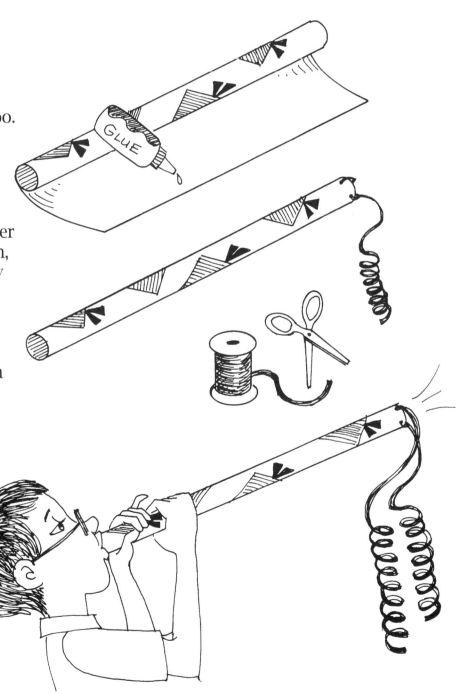

Kazoos

Younger Elementary Children

What You Need

- Toilet paper tubes
- Waxed paper
- Rubber bands
- Pencils
- Birthday gift wrap paper with general design like balloons, party hats, and so forth (not cartoon characters or superheroes)
- Scissors
- White glue or glue sticks

What You Do

1. Show children how to cut the gift wrap and glue it on the toilet paper tube to cover it.

2. Children then cut waxed paper so that it is a few inches larger than the opening of the tube. They put the waxed paper over the open end of the tube and secure it in place with a rubber band.

3. Help each child to use a pencil to carefully poke a hole in the tube about an inch from the end with the waxed paper.

4. To play, children pucker their lips and hum into the open end of the kazoo.

Flowers

In many countries with a cool climate, spring flowers are emphasized on Pentecost rather than on Easter, since more flowers are in bloom.

Pentecost May Baskets

Older Elementary Children

The custom of decorating May baskets for the first day of May can be adapted to Pentecost celebrations that occur at the end of May or the first of June.

What You Need

- Empty, rinsed-out 2-liter plastic milk jugs
- Red poster-board strips, 1"x 12"
- Hole punch
- Brads
- Red acrylic paint
- Paintbrushes
- Red shredded tissue paper
- Florists' clay
- Scissors
- Glue
- Red and white flowers (geraniums, carnations, baby's breath, chrysanthemums, etc.)

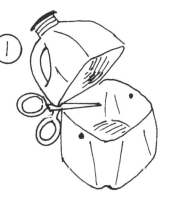
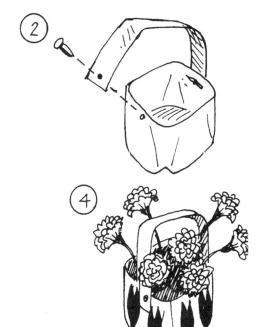

What You Do

1. Show children how to make the basket. With sharp scissors, they cut off the top section of the plastic milk jug and discard it, leaving a basket-shaped plastic section. Use a hole punch to punch two holes equidistant around the edge about one-half inch down from the top.

2. Children can punch a hole about three-quarter inch from both ends of the poster-board strip. They use brads to attach the strip to the milk jug to make a handle.

3. Children can use red acrylic paint to paint flames on the sides of the basket. Set aside to dry.

4. When the paint is dry, children can put some florists' clay in the bottom of the jug. They can put some water in the jug and arrange the red and white flowers.

5. Children can carry the Pentecost baskets in a procession on Pentecost and then take them home for table decorations, or deliver them to church members who are sick or unable to leave their homes or to people in hospitals or nursing homes.

♣ And More . . .

Instead of fresh flowers, fill the basket with dried flowers or red tissue-paper flowers (see p. 40).

Red Tissue-Paper Flowers

Older Elementary Children

What You Need

- Red tissue paper
- Scissors
- 9-inch thin florists' wire
- Ruler

What You Do

1. Have the children cut the tissue paper into nine-inch squares. They then stack six to eight squares on top of each other.

2. Show the children how to fold the stack of squares accordion-style until the entire stack is folded like a fan.

3. In the center of the folded tissue, have the children twist a nine-inch piece of florists' wire.

4. To form the flower, children should separate each piece of tissue paper on both sides of the wire and pull each one up to form petals.

5. Use to decorate the church for a Pentecost service, or as decorations for a Happy Birthday Church party.

♣ And More . . .

Combine red and white tissue or red, yellow, and orange tissue paper to make more colorful flowers.

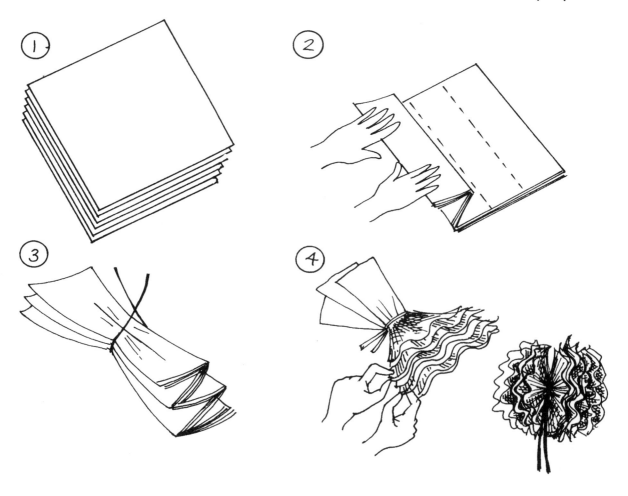

The Church

In *Acts 2:42* we read of the early church:

They devoted themselves to the apostles' teaching and fellowship, to the breaking of bread and the prayers.

And so it is today. The church preaches, teaches, worships, engages in mission, and breaks bread together.

The Early Christian Church

Fish and Other Secret Symbols
• • • • • • • • • • • •

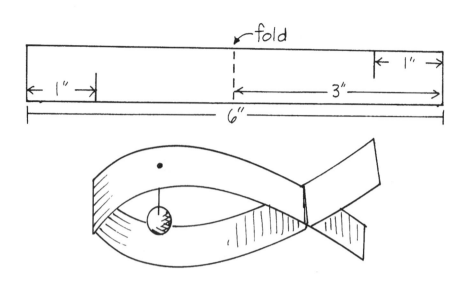

Secret Symbol Mobile

Older Elementary Children

What You Need

- Metal coat hangers
- Strips of heavy colored paper, 1 inch wide
- Scissors
- Yarn or string
- Large needle and heavy white carpet thread
- Small craft beads (optional)

What You Do

1. Tell the children that the first Christians were persecuted by the Roman government. It was so dangerous to be identified as a Christian that followers developed secret signs that only other Christians recognized. They used the same symbols as secret messages to each other drawn on the walls of the catacombs, where they often hid to worship.

2. Explain why the fish was used as a secret symbol (see pp. 47–48). Then draw a Chi Rho for the children. Explain that these are the first two letters of the word *Christ* in Greek. The sign looks like an *X* with a *P* in the center.

3. Show the children how to make a fish with a six-inch strip of paper. One inch from each end, show them how to use scissors to cut two slits, each one halfway through the strip. They then slide the two strips together.

4. Children can add an eye to the fish if they like. Show them how to thread the needle and put a knot in one end. About three-quarters of an inch from the nose end of the fish, they push the needle through the top strip and pull it through until the knot catches at the end. Thread a bead on the thread, pull it up until it hangs down about one-half inch, and make a knot under the bead (be sure the knot is big enough to hold). Cut off the excess thread.

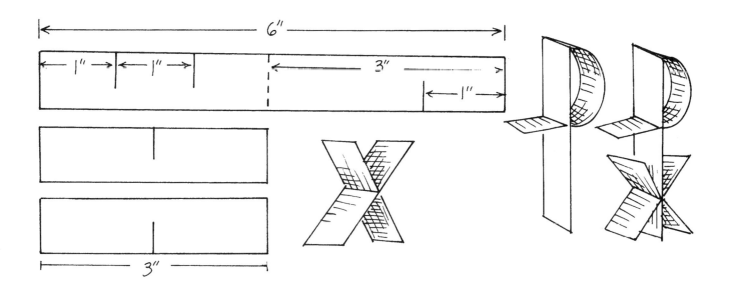

5. For the Chi Rho, children will need two strips about three inches long and one strip six inches long. They slit the short strips in the middle and slide together to form an *X*. Then they slit the long strip about one inch from the end and again two inches from the other end on the left side. They slide the top into the upper slit to form a *P*. Slide the *P* behind the *X*.

6. Children can make several fish and Chi Rhos, and cut yarn at varying lengths to hang the symbols from the coat hanger. Attach yarn to the hanger and hang to display.

Fish Rubbings

Young Children and Younger Elementary Children

What You Need

- Newsprint, typing, or other thin paper, approximately 8" x 10"
- Cardboard templates of fish pattern (see p. 84)
- Paper clips, sandpaper, bricks or concrete blocks, other textured projects or surfaces
- Crayons, with paper peeled off
- Masking tape
- 8 1/2" x 11" colored construction paper
- Glue

What You Do

1. Secure the cardboard fish templates to the tabletop with masking tape. Show the children how to put the paper on top of the template and rub lightly with the side of a crayon over the paper until the shape of the fish appears.

2. Children can place paper clips or other textured objects under the paper and rub with a darker-colored crayon to make fish scales or other markings. They can also put their papers on a concrete-block wall, over bricks, or even over the soles of their running shoes to get interesting textures for their fish bodies.

3. Use glue to mount the children's fish rubbings on colored construction paper.

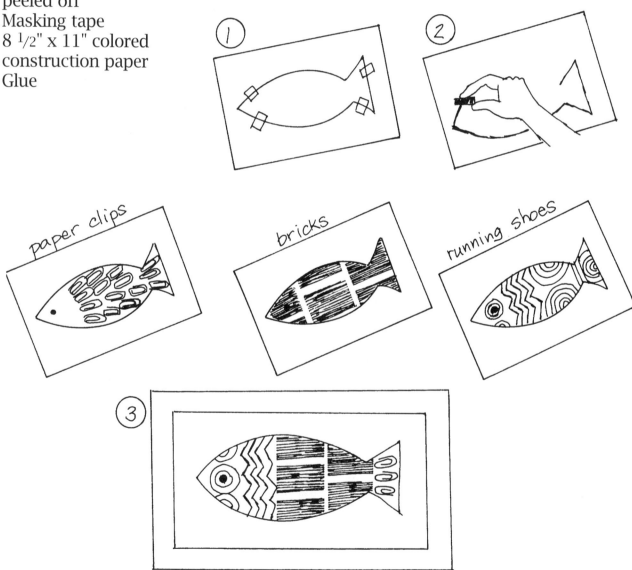

44

Batik Fish

Older Elementary Children

What You Need

- Pieces of muslin, about 9" x 12" (one for each child)
- Artists' charcoal sticks
- Old newspapers
- Masking tape
- Paraffin (purchased in a hobby and craft store or a grocery store)
- Old crayons, with paper peeled off
- Old electric frying pan, lined with aluminum foil
- Clean tuna or cat food cans
- Paintbrushes
- Large dye pot
- Cold-water dye (such as Rit or Putnam)
- Sink for rinsing
- Iron
- Clothesline and clothespins
- Needle and thread
- 12-inch dowel sticks

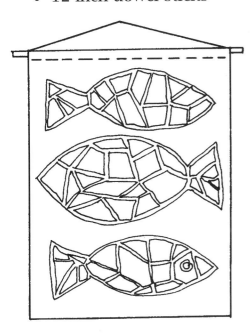

What You Do

1. Melt paraffin in cans in an electric frying pan lined with foil. Add peeled crayons to make several colors. This forms a mixture of hot wax.

2. Explain the reason for the use of the fish symbol and its significance (see pp. 47-48).

3. Using artists' charcoal, the children can lightly sketch on the muslin a fish shape and any details they wish to add (Greek letters for *fish, scales, eyes*, etc.)

4. Tape the muslin to a pad made of several layers of newspaper. Children can then use paintbrushes to paint hot wax on the muslin using the fish shape they sketched previously as a guide.

5. When all the wax has been applied, show children how to crackle the wax by crushing the muslin.

6. Put the muslin in the pot of dye and let soak for ten minutes.

7. Tell children to rinse the muslin in the sink and hang it to dry on a clothesline.

8. When the cloth is dry, place it between several layers of newspaper and press until all the wax is removed and absorbed in the newspaper, changing newspapers as necessary.

9. Fold down the top of the batik and sew a casing with needle and thread. Now the batiks can be displayed by sliding a dowel through the casing and suspending.

✤ And More . . .

—Sew all the completed batiks together to make one large banner.
—Show children how to take a plain muslin square of the same size as the batik and put the wrong sides of the two pieces of fabric together. Secure with straight pins. Show children how to stitch the two pieces together on three sides, turn right side out, and stuff with batting. Children can then sew the fourth side closed to make a pillow.

String-Weaving Fish

Older Elementary Children

What You Need:

- Heavy twine
- Yarn (several colors)
- Heavy wire (coat-hanger wire)
- Craft beads
- Large embroidery needles

What You Do

1. Show the children how to bend the heavy wire to make a simple fish shape.

2. Show them how to tie a knot securing one end of the heavy twine to the wire form. They then wrap the twine around the form, completely covering it, and knotting the twine at the end. They then use the needles to thread yarn back and forth across the fish shape at about three-quarter inch intervals to form the wuff threads for weaving.

3. Now children are ready to weave. They can use their fingers to weave over-under-over-under, or they can use the needle as a shuttle. When they change yarn colors or come to the end of a piece of yarn, they should overlap the next piece about one inch.

4. As children reach the midpoint of weaving, they can thread a craft bead onto the yarn to add an eye.

5. Children can experiment with looping the yarn to make scales.

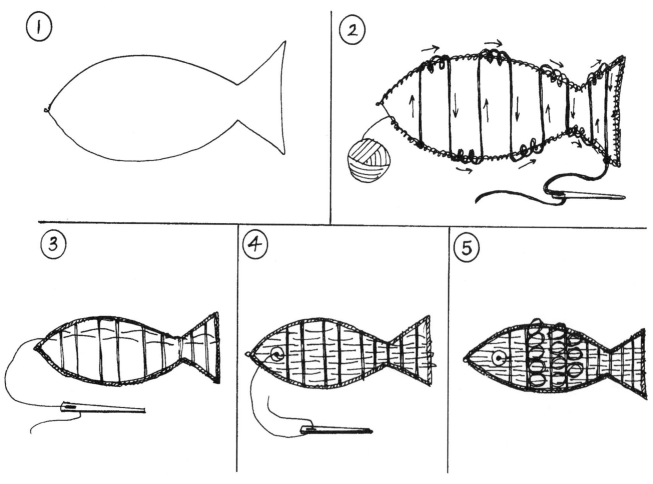

Things To Do

●●●●●●●●●●●●

Worship in Hiding

Older Elementary Children

What You Need

- "Christians in Rome" (see p. 49)
- Signs of the fish (see this page)

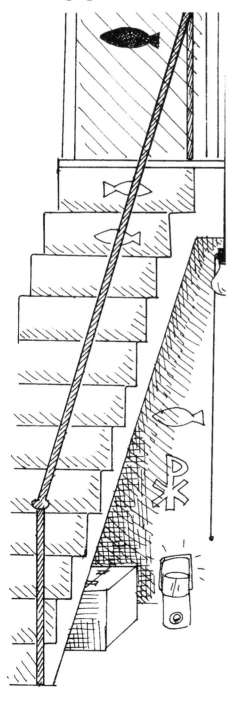

What You Do

1. Ask the children: What would we do if the government forbade us to worship together? Do you know of any place where this has happened? (Older children may mention Nazi Germany and its persecution of the Jews, or some communist countries where people were formerly not allowed to gather to worship.)

2. Tell the children that early Christians in Rome were in a similar situation. Then read the account "Christians in Rome."

3. Ask the children: How do we know when a service of worship is happening in our church? List the places we might find out about it:

   —signboard in front of church
   —announcements in public service of worship
   —notices in the religion section of our newspaper
   —announcements in our church newsletter
   —announcements on the radio or TV

Say to the children: Suppose you had been a Christian in Rome. How would you find out where Christians were worshiping together? Let the children suggest ways the Christians might have communicated with each other. Then say: Christians had a special symbol that reminded them of Jesus. It was the fish.

Draw a simple fish outline on chalkboard or newsprint. Say to the children: The Greek letters ΙΧΟΥΣ spell "fish." They are also the first letters of the Greek words meaning "Jesus Christ, Son of God, Savior":

I = Jesus
CH = Christ
TH = of God
U = Son
S = Savior

While the fish reminded Christians of Jesus, it made the Romans think of funerals. So when Christians painted a fish on the wall near their place of worship, their enemies thought the visitors to that room were going to a funeral. Instead, they were meeting to worship God and teach one another about Jesus.

The fish reminded Christians of Jesus' disciples who were fishers. When one person met another, he or she would make a simple drawing of a fish in the sand with the toe of one foot. If the other person recognized the design, he or she knew they were both Christians.

4. Plan a worship service. You will want to include the following elements that were a part of the early church's worship:

> Call to worship
> Prayer of thanksgiving to God for Jesus Christ
> Hymn (*Old Testament psalms*)
> Reading of the Scriptures
>   (the early Christians had only the Old Testament)
> Sermon (*about Jesus' life, death, and
>   resurrection*)
> Reading of a letter (*when Paul wrote letters,
>   they were read as a part of the service*)
> The Lord's Supper
> Benediction

5. Choose a secret place to have your worship service. Some possibilities are a furnace room, an out-of-the-way storage area, or a corner of a church balcony. (Be sure to clear the use of the space with your church governing body.) Mark the way to the worship place with simple fish drawings. Plan to light the space with candles (if fire regulations permit) or flashlights. Do not use any more light than this. Do not set up chairs. In this way children can get a sense of worshiping in an uncomfortable space.

6. When you are ready to have the worship service, gather in your usual group space. Read "Christians in Rome" (p. 49). Then tell the children that they are to imagine that they are early Christians. To worship safely, they must make their way in secret to the worship place. Divide the group into twos and threes and ask a young person or adult to go with each group. At intervals let each group follow the fish signs to the worship space.

7. When the worship is over, have the small groups leave at different intervals.

Christians in Rome

At first, the Romans thought the Christians had the same religion as the Jews. Paul was a Jew, and Jesus, whose gospel Paul preached, had been a Jew. Rome was used to the Jews. Jews worship their one God in synagogues, and they were the only people in the Roman Empire who were not compelled to burn incense to the Roman emperor. But the Christians soon showed that they were different. There were more Gentiles than Jews among them. Not only did they refuse to worship the Roman emperor, but they would not follow other Roman customs. "We must look into this," said the Romans. So Christians were spied on, and many foolish and untrue stories about them were passed around from one person to another.

Once a fire broke out in Rome. It burned for a week and almost destroyed the whole city. Nero (the emperor) said that the Christians started the fire, so many of them were nailed to crosses and burned. Up on the hill, in the garden of his palace, Nero watched these human torches light up the night sky.

This was the beginning of a terrible persecution of the Christians in Rome. It is not certain just when Paul died, but we do know that when the day came, he went without fear to give his life to Jesus Christ.

For a long time things looked very dark for the church. Men, women, and children were forced to hide, and no home in the city was safe. The Christians took refuge in underground caves and tunnels in the outskirts of Rome.

In times of persecution, Christians went creeping along these narrow, winding passages, some as deep as seventy feet below the surface, to their secret places for worship. The pale light of a lamp flickered over their tired faces as the leader read from the Scriptures and prayed that God would help them to stand fast in these dreadful tests of their faith. As they broke bread together and drank from the cup of wine, they gained comfort and strength. On the walls of these caves the Christians painted pictures that stood for their beliefs. Many of these pictures became symbols that are seen in our church today.

49

In the Catacombs

Older Elementary Children

Check with appliance stores a month before you plan to set up the catacombs and ask if large boxes can be saved for you.

What You Need

- Appliance boxes (10 to 20)
- Duct tape or stove bolts
- Box cutters or sharp knives
- Tempera paint
- Paint brushes
- Empty classroom space for setting up the tunnel

What You Do

1. Read "Christians in Rome" (p. 49) to the children. Explain that they will be constructing a tunnel made of appliance boxes so that they can imagine what it was like for early Christians who traveled secretly in tunnels and passageways.

2. Let the children decide how to set up their tunnel. Some boxes can be set on their sides so that the children must crawl through them. Others can be upright.

3. Before putting the tunnel together, let the children paint Christian symbols, such as the fish or the Chi Rho (see pp. 42-43), on the insides of the boxes.

4. Connect all the boxes by using stove bolts or duct tape. You will need to cut holes in the sides of the boxes you are using in the upright position. If you do this by cutting a large X, the sides can be folded back and taped to the next box (see below).

5. At the end of the tunnel, have a space set up for an early Christian worship service (see p. 48).

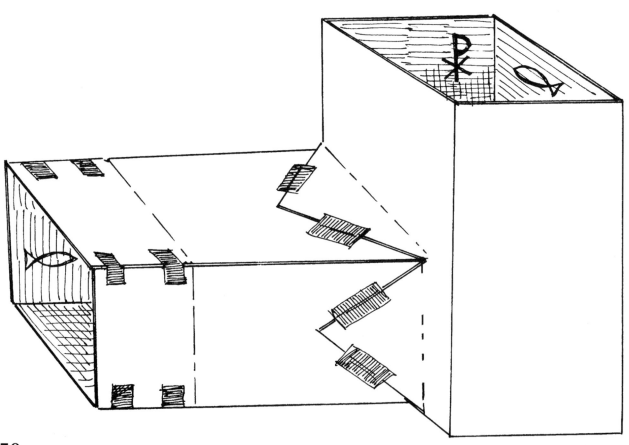

"In the Name of Jesus" Echo Drama

Younger Elementary Children

What You Need

- Echo Drama (pp. 52-53)

What You Do

1. Talk with the children about names. Mention some common expressions such as, "I don't want my name associated with that." How do children feel when there is name calling? Note that in the Lord's Prayer we say, "Hallowed be thy name."

2. Ask, What does it mean when we end a prayer by saying, "In Jesus' name . . . "? Tell the children: In the time of Jesus and in the time of the very first church, a name meant a great deal. If someone did a thing *in the name of Jesus*, it meant that Jesus would have done exactly that. This is a story about the name of Jesus and how much it meant.

3. Read aloud the Echo Drama on pages 52-53, pausing after each line to let the children repeat the words and actions.

4. Talk with the children about what it means today to do something *in the name of Jesus*. What kinds of things might they do? How might they treat other people in the name of Jesus?

Echo Drama

At the gate called Beautiful a lame man sat.
    (*Fold arms over body*)
"Money! Money! Give money to a poor lame man!"
    (*Cup hands over mouth and call out*)
One day Peter and John went up to the Temple to pray.
    (*Fold hands as if praying*)
"Money! Money! Give money to a poor lame man!"
    (*Cup hands over mouth and call out*)
"Look at us!" said Peter.
    (*Point to self*)
"Silver and gold have I none,"
    (*Shake head from side to side*)

52

"But what I have, I give to you."
"In the name of Jesus of Nazareth, stand up and walk!"
    (*Stretch out hands*)
Peter took the man by the right hand, and raised him up.
    (*Stretch hand down, then slowly raise as if helping man up*)
Jumping up, he stood and began to walk.
    (*Jump up and walk in place*)
And he entered the Temple, walking and
  leaping and praising God,
    (*Walk and leap in place*)
All the people saw him walking and praising God,
    (*Raise arm and point*)
And they were filled with wonder and amazement at
  what had happened to him.
    (*Look amazed*)

The Church Today

The Church at Home

· · · · · · · · · · ·

Billboard for Your Church

Older Elementary Children

This activity will help your children put in words what they think is special about their own congregation.

What You Need

- Newsprint and markers
- Sheets of poster board (one for each child)
- Colored felt-tipped markers
- Lightweight sticks about 3 feet long (optional)
- Masking tape

What You Do

1. With the children, brainstorm a list of things that they think makes your congregation unique. What do the children like best about their church?

2. On another sheet of newsprint, talk with the children about what other people need to know about the church: when to come, what will happen, who will preach, and what special programs are available.

3. Let each child make a "billboard" on a sheet of poster board advertising your congregation.

4. Display the posters in a hallway, or attach lightweight sticks to the backs of the posters with tape and line a sidewalk outside your church building with the posters.

Sponge-Print People at Church

Young Children

What You Need

- Large piece of mural or butcher paper
- Large sponges cut into "people" using the pattern on p. 81
- Two to three colors of tempera paint, mixed with a little liquid dishwashing detergent
- Aluminum pie pans, or other shallow flat pans
- Black felt-tipped markers
- Church pattern (see p. 82)

What You Do

1. In advance, use the church pattern on p. 82 to draw a large church outline on the mural paper. If you like, alter the pattern to resemble more closely your own church building.

2. Pour the tempera paint mixed with a little dishwashing detergent into the flat pans. Slightly dampen the sponge people. Let the children dip them in the tempera paint, then print the shape of a person on the mural paper next to the church.

3. Children can print people shapes all around the church outline and even inside.

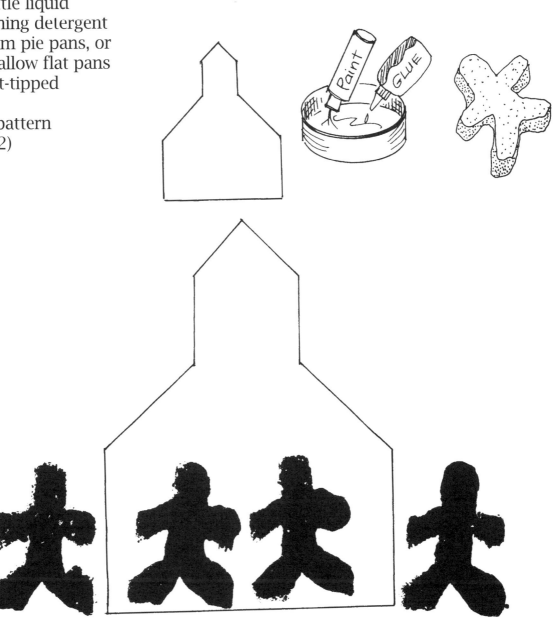

Paper-Doll People of the Church

Younger Elementary Children

Use these paper dolls to "people" a church bulletin board.

What You Need

- White paper, approximately 8" x 16"
- Scissors
- Crayons or colored felt-tipped markers
- Scraps of construction paper, wallpaper sample, fabric scraps, yarn, other scrap materials to decorate the dolls
- Cardboard templates cut from people pattern on p. 81

What You Do

1. Show the children how to fold the paper accordion-style as shown below. Children then trace around the template on the top side of the folded paper.

2. Show the children how to cut out the paper dolls. Be sure they understand not to cut on the dotted line on the fold.

3. Children then unfold the dolls and lay them flat to decorate. Encourage each child to make one doll that looks like him or her, then to decorate the other three dolls in the strip to resemble people in their church.

4. Attach the dolls to a mural of your church building.

The Church Is People (Bulletin Board)

Young Children and Younger Elementary Children

What You Need

- Large piece of mural or butcher paper
- Church pattern (see p. 82)
- 8 ¹/₂" x 11" construction paper
- Black felt-tipped marker
- Camera and film (preferably an instant-developing camera)

What You Do

1. Talk with the children about people who make up your church and do important work. List the names of the church staff, church school teachers, governing board members, and others the children know.

2. Decide which members you will photograph. The children's choices may not be those members considered important by the adults.

3. Arrange to take pictures of the church members the children chose. Let the children ask each person to name one thing he or she likes about your church. Have one child record these responses next to each person's name.

4. Give each child one or two pictures. Show children how to fold the construction paper in half to make a folder. On one side, the child can glue the picture. Under the picture, the child can print the person's name. On the other side of the folder, the child can print the person's response to the question about your church.

5. Attach the folders to the mural on which you have drawn the large church outline made by the church pattern (or your own line drawing). The folders will resemble church windows with shutters.

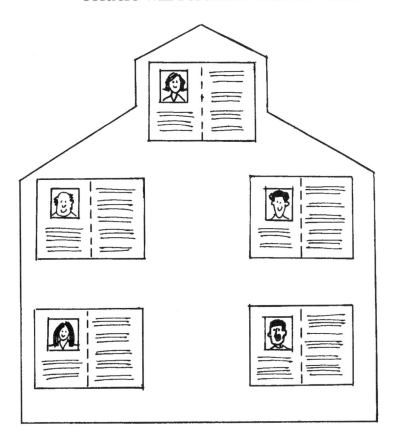

"We Are One in the Spirit" Banner

Children of All Ages

You can make a more permanent banner by using muslin squares.

What You Need

- 8 1/2" x 11" white construction paper
- Colored felt-tipped markers
- Hole punch
- Red ribbon or yarn
- Scissors
- Red poster board, 3 or 4 sheets
- Dowel stick or curtain rod about 6 feet long

What You Do

1. Give each child a piece of white construction paper. Ask children: What do you think is special about you? What gifts do you have that you can use in the church for God's realm? Ask each child to draw a picture on the paper that shows his or her special contribution to the church.

2. Invite some older children who are finished with their pictures to help you make a banner header. Invite the children to decide how they want the title to read. They might want the words "We are" and "in the Spirit" to be horizontal and the word "one" to be larger and to hang vertically, or they might want the word "Spirit" to look like a flame. Cut out letters from white construction paper and glue them on the red poster board. Then cut the poster board so that each word is on a separate piece of poster board. Punch two holes in the top of each piece, attach yarn to the holes, and hang the words from the dowel or curtain rod.

3. Punch holes in the bottom edge of each piece of poster board, attach yarn, and add the children's drawings. Add additional drawings to the bottom edges of the first row.

4. Hang the banner where it can be enjoyed by the congregation.

Church Dinner Place Mats

Younger and Older Elementary Children

Start by making place mats identifying particular church school classes, the church staff, members of the governing board, or church school teachers. Expand it to include all the church members or all families in the church if you are ambitious!

What You Need

- 12" x 18" colored construction paper
- Camera and film (preferably an instant-developing camera)
- Copies of the "Yes, We're the Church Together" form (see p. 60)
- Glue
- Fine-lined black markers
- Clear, self-adhesive shelf liner (or laminating machine and film
- Crayons or colored markers

What You Do

1. Let the children decide who will be depicted on the place mats. (In advance, check with the "targeted" people to arrange interview times.)

2. Let children work in twos or in small groups to ask the questions on the form and fill out the information. Be on hand to take a picture of the interviewee during the interview, or let one child do the photographing.

3. Children can glue the person's photo and the form on a sheet of construction paper. They can use crayons or colored markers to decorate the paper.

4. Cover each place mat with clear, self-adhesive shelf liner, or have them laminated.

5. Use the place mats at a church dinner.

Yes, We're the Church Together

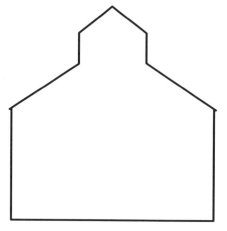

My name is _____

In our church, I_____

_____

One thing I like best about our church is_____

_____

My favorite hymn is_____

_____

My favorite story about Jesus is_____

_____

Here is a passage from the Bible that has meaning for me:_____

_____

_____

Church Family Tree

Older Elementary Children

What You Need

- Large sheet of butcher or mural paper
- Pictures of people or events from your congregation's history
- Index cards
- Felt-tipped markers
- Church historian or someone else to talk about your church history
- Stapler or tape

What You Do

1. Invite the church historian or a church member who can talk about your church's history to visit and talk to the children. Explain to that person that you will be making a church family tree.

2. On the mural paper, make a large outline of a tree. As the church member talks, children can make index cards that briefly list important events or the names of important people in your church's history, such as the date the church was founded, or when the church building was completed, or the name of the first pastor of your church.

3. Attach the index cards to the tree outline with tape or a stapler. Include any picture of people or events.

The Church Near and Far

● ● ● ● ● ● ● ● ● ● ●

"Sing Allelu" Box Montage

Younger and Older Elementary Children

What You Need

- "Sing Allelu" poem on this page
- Large appliance box
- Photographs of people from all races and cultures (*National Geographic* magazine, old curriculum materials, or mission resources from your denomination)
- Scissors
- Mixture of white glue and water
- Paintbrushes
- Poster board on which poem is printed

What You Do

1. Say the poem "Sing Allelu" below. Talk with the children about the church around the world.

2. Show the children how to cut out pictures, lay them on three sides of the appliance box, and paint over them with the glue and water mixture. They should overlap the pictures slightly.

3. On the fourth side of the box, glue a sheet of poster board on which children have printed the poem. Children can then glue more pictures of people around the poem.

Sing Allelu

The people of the church
   Are many different colors.
We're many different ages,
   We're big and little, too!
The people of the church
   Are born to love each other.
We are the church—
Sing Allelu!

The people of the church
   Live in many different places.
All around the world
   There are churches old and new.
The people of the church
   Are born to love each other!
We are the church—
Sing Allelu!

♣ **And More . . .**

Make the poem into an illustrated choral reading. Let individual children or small groups illustrate a single line on poster board by making a picture montage. For example, one child could do a montage of people of different races, another could illustrate people of different ages, and so forth. To do the choral reading, have the child or group who illustrated the line read it. Everyone repeats the final two lines in each stanza ("We are the church—Sing Allelu!")

Suitcase Collage

Younger Elementary Children

What You Need

- Brown wrapping paper cut according to the suitcase pattern on p. 83
- Magazine pictures of food, clothing, and other things people need
- World map or globe
- Scissors
- Glue
- Heavy twine or rope, cut in 8-inch lengths
- Masking tape
- Mission materials on areas of need

What You Do

1. Talk with the children about the things people in the world need. If there is a particular country or area of the world currently in the news where you know people are experiencing famine or water shortage or where there are refugees, locate that place on a map or globe and talk about what is going on there. Use any mission materials you have been able to obtain about that area of the world to talk about what the church is doing to help.

2. Give each child a paper suitcase. Tell the children that they are to find pictures of things people need in order to live and glue them in their suitcases. If children cannot locate a picture they would like to include, they can draw one.

3. Give each child a length of rope to tape to the top of the suitcase as a handle.

"Give Us This Day Our Daily Bread" Box

Younger and Older Elementary Children

This box uses the montage technique.

What You Need

- "Church People Help People Who Are Hungry" poem on this page
- White index cards
- Pictures of bread cut from magazines
- Small cardboard boxes with lids (one for each child)
- Mixture of white glue and water
- Paintbrushes
- Sharp scissors

What You Do

1. Show children how to place pictures on the box and paint over them with the glue and water mixture. They can cover three sides of the box with pictures of bread.

2. Let children copy the verse onto an index card and glue to the fourth side of the box. They can add pictures to cover space not covered by the card.

3. Then they can decorate the lid of the box. Set aside the box and lid to dry.

4. Show children how to use a pair of sharp scissors to cut a slit in the lid of the box (younger children may need your help). Make the slit large enough for coins to slip through easily.

5. Encourage the children to take the box home and place it on the table. Family members can put in a coin every time they eat a slice of bread or something containing fiber.

6. When the box is full, it can be brought to the church and given to the pastor to be donated to a hunger project.

Church People Help People Who Are Hungry

Thank you, God, for your love and care,
 for all your children everywhere.
As we receive our daily bread,
 there are others who must be fed.
May hands stretch out both near
 and far
 to offer bread where the hungry are.
Help us give your love and care
 to all your children, everywhere.

64

The Church That Love Built

Older Elementary Children

This is an ongoing project.

What You Need

- Large cardboard carton
- Sheet of cardboard 1 1/2 times as large as the top of the large box
- Old magazines and catalogs (for pictures of all kinds of people and of scenes from nature)
- Mixture of white glue and water
- Paintbrushes
- Scissors
- Colored felt-tipped markers
- 4" x 6" white index cards (or pieces of poster board cut 4" x 6")
- Poster board
- Tape

What You Do

1. Tell the children that over the next few sessions, you will be building a church. Ask children: What do you think keeps the church together? Tell them that the church is held together by God's love for us and by our love for God and for one another. When they have finished building their church they will be able to see what kind of church we would have if we learned to live in obedience to God and with kindness and generosity to our neighbors.

2. First, give the children magazines and catalogs and tell them to look for pictures of things that God can create that we humans cannot. They can tear out the pictures and trim them with scissors. Show them how to place a picture on the outside of the carton and paint over it with the mixture of glue and water. They should slightly overlap the pictures. Phrases or words could also be added. Children should cover all four sides of the outside of the carton.

3. In this step, fold the sheet of cardboard in half. On one half, have a child print "New Testament" in large letters. Another child can print the words "Old Testament" on the other half. Tell the children that this will be the roof of the church. It reminds us that the Bible is the book of the church. Children can use markers to print Bible verses on the cardboard.

4. Next, the children will cover the inside of the carton with pictures of all kinds of human beings, using the same technique that they used with the outside of the carton. Turn the carton over or open the top so that they can reach inside easily. When the sides are covered and the glue is dry, cut a large door on one side of the carton. Fold it back so the insides of the carton can be seen. Put the "roof" constructed in step 3 on top of the church building.

5. Finally, children can use colored markers on index cards to draw pictures of children working together doing kind or generous acts. Tape the cards together to form a pathway to the church door. Tell the children that the church community works inside and outside the church to minister to neighbors.

6. Make a poster describing The Church That Love Built. Display the church and the poster together where other members of the congregation can see it.

Things To Do

The Church Remembers

Older Elementary Children

What You Need

- List of interview questions (see this page)
- Tape recorder or video camera
- Two or three older members of the church who are willing to be interviewed
- Bible

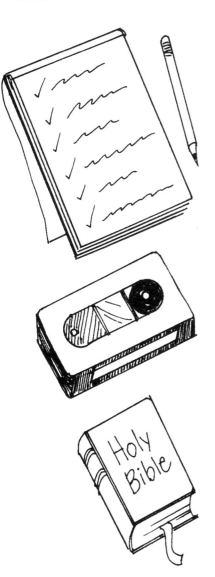

What You Do

1. Read aloud *Acts 2* for the children. Tell them that it is the story of the beginning of the church and that today they will be adding to the story of the church by interviewing people who can tell them more about the beginning of your particular congregation.

2. Let the children decide who will ask each of the questions of the older members who have agreed to be interviewed. Add to the list any additional questions the children may want to ask. If you are using a video camera, decide who will operate the camera and be sure that child knows how to operate the equipment.

3. Encourage the children to ask their questions clearly, speaking slowly so that the question will be picked up on the audiotape or videotape.

Interview Questions:

1. When was this church founded?
2. Where did the people meet for worship?
3. When was the first building dedicated?
4. How big was the congregation?
5. Who was the first minister?
6. Who has been a member here the longest?
7. What is your earliest memory about this church?
8. Is there a story about something that happened to this church that you would like to share?
   (*Let the children add any other questions they would like to add.*)

♣ And More . . .

If the children are making a videotape, incorporate photographs or memorabilia about the church's history. Let the older members who are being interviewed describe the photos or other items on camera.

"How the Church Grows" Guessing Game

Younger Elementary Children

This game uses an old traditional children's game "Dollar, Dollar."

What You Need

- "How the Church Grows" poem, p. 69
- Photocopied Scriptures (see p. 70) cut apart and folded in half (add additional Scripture, if you like)
- Small cross necklace, wooden cross, or a small cross cut from cardboard (small enough to be concealed in a child's hand)
- Small basket or box

What You Do

1. Have the children sit on the floor in a circle with their hands in their laps, capping the left hand in the right hand.

2. Explain that as you say and repeat the verse, the children are to move their left hand from their own cupped hand to the cupped hand of the child to their left.

3. Give one child the cross and tell him or her to conceal it in the hand. Tell the children that they are to try to move the cross from hand to hand without letting anyone see where it is. Practice moving the cross around the circle as you repeat the verse.

4. Choose one child to be "it." "It" sits in the center of the circle while the children move the cross from hand. "It" tries to see whose hand is concealing the cross. When you have finished reciting the verse, "it" gets three chances to guess where the cross is. When "it" guesses correctly, he or she gets to choose a Scripture paper from the basket and read it aloud.

5. The child who is holding the cross then becomes "it."

6. Continue playing the game until everyone has had a turn and all the verses have been read. If you have more children than there are passages, return the papers to the basket to be read again.

7. Talk with the children about how they might share the good news of God's love with other people. What other ways might we do this besides sharing the words of the Bible? How can we show people God's love?

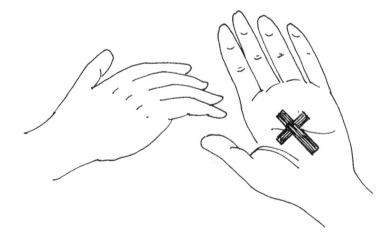

How the Church Grows

One friend told another that Jesus loved him.
That friend told some others that Jesus cares.
The others listened . . .
They heard about Jesus
And spread the good news to friends of theirs.
One friend to another! That's how it grows,
And all around the world, most everyone knows
That God's Word and your word is
How the church grows!

—Marjorie Anderson Smith,
Children at Home

- -

For God so loved the world that he gave his only Son, so that everyone who believes in him may not perish but may have eternal life. (*John 3:16*)

- -

The LORD is my shepherd, I shall not want.
 He makes me lie down in green pastures;
he leads me beside still waters;
 he restores my soul.
He leads me in right paths for his
 name's sake.

(*Ps. 23:1–3*)

- -

"Go therefore and make disciples of all nations, baptizing them in the name of the Father and of the Son and of the Holy Spirit, and teaching them to obey everything that I have commanded you. And remember, I am with you always, to the end of the age." (*Matt. 28:19–20*)

- -

"For the promise is for you, for your children, and for all who are far away, everyone whom the Lord our God calls to him." (*Acts 2:39*)

- -

For I am convinced that neither death, nor life, nor angels, nor rulers, nor things present, nor things to come, nor powers, nor height, nor depth, nor anything else in all creation, will be able to separate us from the love of God in Christ Jesus our Lord. (*Rom. 8:38–39*)

- -

For just as the body is one and has many members, and all the members of the body, though many, are one body, so it is with Christ. (*1 Cor. 12:12*)

- -

There is no longer Jew or Greek, there is no longer slave or free, there is no longer male and female; for all of you are one in Christ Jesus. (*Gal. 3:28*)

- -

A Numbers Game

Young Children

This is a good game to play with young children and first-graders who are just learning something about numbers. The game is patterned after "The Farmer in the Dell."

What You Need

- "Numbers Rhyme" on this page

What You Do

1. Say the "Numbers Rhyme" below, pausing to let children fill in the appropriate number.

2. Have the children form a circle. Choose one child to be in the center of the circle. Sing the verse to the tune of "Farmer in the Dell" and let children choose others to join them in the circle (one chooses a second, those two choose two more, and so forth until there are eight). Finish the song.

3. Choose another child to be in the center of the circle and continue playing until everyone has had a chance to be in the circle.

Numbers Rhyme

One person told the other,
    "God loves you."
When one person tells another
    That makes _____.
Two people get excited
    And tell two more;
When two tell two others
    That makes _____.
Four people told four others—
    The news couldn't wait—
Told their fathers and their mothers;
    Now there were _____.

The news has traveled a long, long way.
People still tell about God's love today.
Who can you tell? And what can you say?
Tell someone about God's love today.

—Marjorie Anderson Smith,
Children at Home

71

"The Church Is Here, The Church Is There" Action Rhyme

Young Children and Younger Elementary Children

What You Need

- Action rhyme on this page

What You Do

1. Repeat the following action rhyme for the children:

   The church is here,
   (*Stand in place*)
   The church is there.
   (*Take one giant step forward*)
   The church is people everywhere!
   (*Join hands and spin around in a circle*)
   Wherever we gather,
   (*Stand in place, arm around friend's waist*)
   Whenever we roam,
   (*Walk away from friend*)
   The church is people
   (*Return to friend, shake hands*)
   Who feel at home!
   (*Friends join hands and spin around in circle*)

2. Ask children to name things we do when we gather together in the church building. They will probably think of praying, reading the Bible, singing, eating together.

3. Then ask them if they know what people of the church do when they are not in the church building. Remind them that people of the church help sick people and people who are hungry. Younger elementary children may know of mission projects in which your church is involved.

4. Ask the children to repeat the rhyme with you again, this time thinking of the things you have discussed as they do the actions.

What Is the Church?

Young Children and Younger Elementary Children

Use this activity along with the making of any of the church murals suggested in this book.

What You Need

- Two fingerplays on this page
- Newsprint and markers (use a completed church mural with people, if you have done one of the church mural-making activities suggested in this book)

What You Do

1. Teach the children the following fingerplay (some may already know it):

    Here is the church
      (*Fold hands, fingers inside*)
    Here is the steeple
      (*Raise two index fingers*)
    Open the door
      (*Open thumbs to show finger "people"*)
    See all the people.

    —Traditional

2. Then teach the children this variation:

    You could have a church
      (*Fold hands, fingers inside*)
    Without any steeple
      (*Shake head from side to side*)
    But you can't have a church
      (*Open thumbs to show finger "people"*)
    Without any people.

    —Pauline Palmer Meek

3. Talk together about people in your own church that the children know. Name the church staff, church school teachers, parents, and children, including the children in the group. If you have completed a church mural with people, point to the people the children put in the mural. Otherwise, list the names of people on newsprint.

4. Tell the children that the people who come to the church building to work, worship God, and learn about the church are what makes the church the church.

♣ And More . . .
Print the words to the rhymes on the door of a completed church mural.

73

"Hurry, Scurry" Action Rhyme

Young Children

What You Need

- Action rhyme on this page

What You Do

1. Teach the children the following action rhyme:

> Hurry, scurry, off we go
> *(Walk fingers)*
> To the church—now don't be slow!
> Friends are waiting, one, two, three,
> *(Count on fingers)*
> And my teacher waits for me.
> Songs to sing and work to do,
> Blocks to build and stories, too.
> *(Pantomime blockbuilding;*
> *hold make-believe book)*
> Sharing toys and showing love,
> *(Fold hands over heart)*
> Giving thanks to God above.
> *(Fold hands in prayer)*
> Jesus loves me, this I know.
> *(Cross hands over chest)*
> Hurry, scurry, off we go.
> *(Walk fingers)*

—Betty McLaney

2. After the children are familiar with the rhyme, repeat just the first four lines. Then say this:

> Many, many things to do
> Guess which one I show to you?

Then choose a child to act out something the children do at church, while the others try to guess.

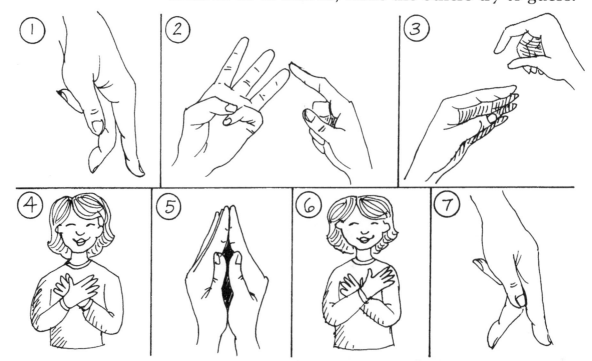

74

God's Love in Any Language

Older Elementary Children

This activity uses the folded paper cootie catcher often made by children of this age.

What You Need

- "God's Love" poem on this page
- Photocopies of "'God Loves Me' in Other Languages" (see p. 76)
- White or colored copy paper 8 ¹/₂" x 11"

What You Do

1. Tell children to use the paper to fold a cootie catcher. Many children (especially girls) will already know how to do this, but follow the diagram below if they need help.

2. Tell children to choose four of the six languages printed, cut out the phrases, and paste them inside the flaps of the catcher. On the top flap they can print which language is underneath.

3. Have children choose a partner to do the activity. Children then slide their fingers inside the catcher. They recite the poem "God's Love" as they move the sections back and forth. When they finish the poem, a partner chooses one of the languages on the top flap, and the other child tries to say the phrase "God loves me" in that language.

❧ And More . . .

See how many languages are spoken in your congregation. Ask members to print in their own language the phrase "God loves me" on a piece of paper and identify the language. Make cootie catchers that use these languages.

God's Love

The church is wherever you are,
The church is wherever you go!
The church is all around the world—
God's love is wherever you go!

—Marjorie Anderson Smith,
Children at Home

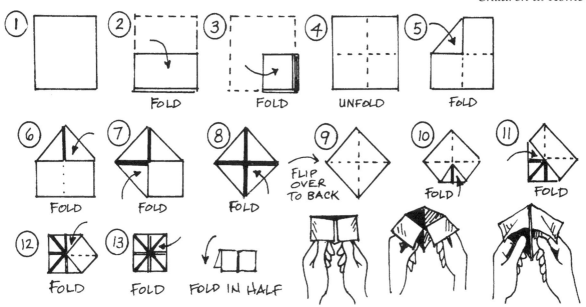

"God Loves Me" in Other Languages

Dieu m'aime (French)
(Dyur m'émé)

Dios me ama (Spanish)
(Dee-os may ahmah)

Gott liebt mich (German)
(Got leebt mick)

나님은 나를 사랑해요. (Korean)
(Ha-na-nim eun Na reul Sah rang yo)

Nzambi udi munnanga (Tshiluba)
(In-zam-bi oo-di moo-nahng-a)

أَلَّهُ يَحُبُّنُ يـ (Arabic)
(Allah you'haybownie)

PATTERNS

Dove

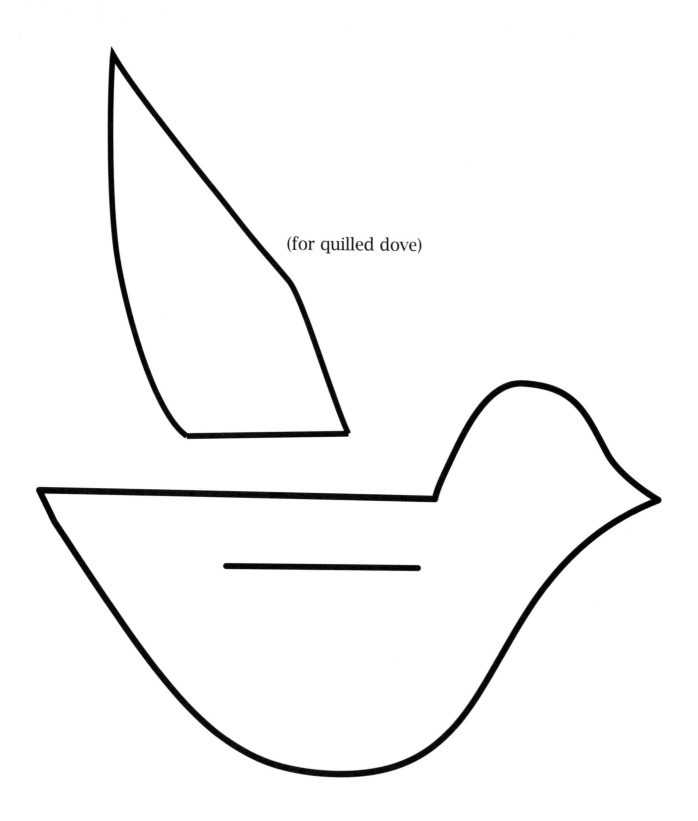

(for quilled dove)

Flame

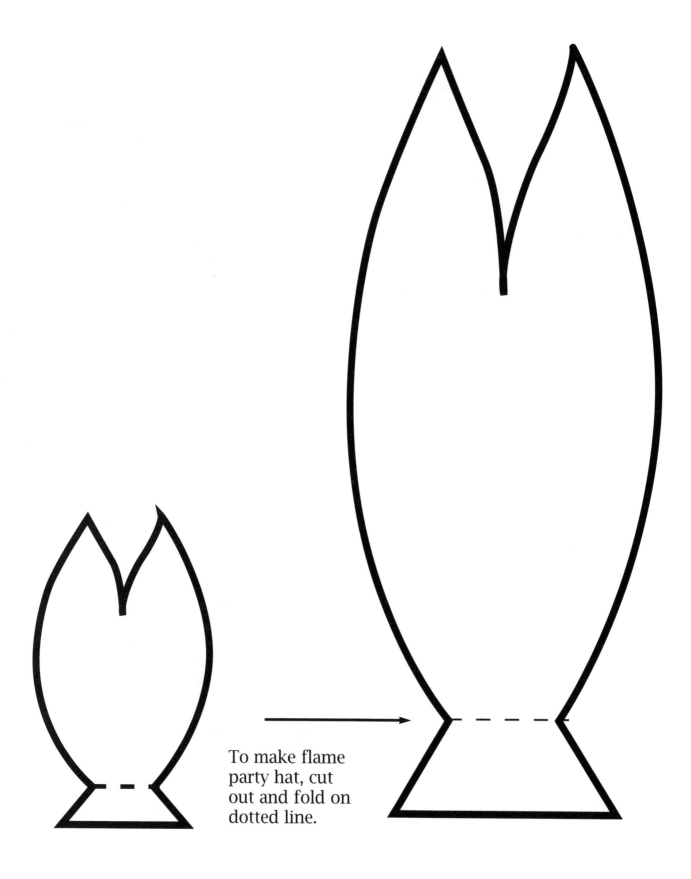

To make flame
party hat, cut
out and fold on
dotted line.

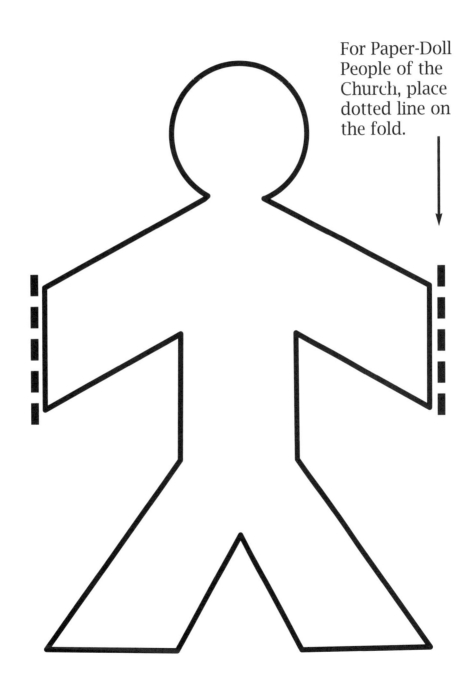

For Paper-Doll
People of the
Church, place
dotted line on
the fold.

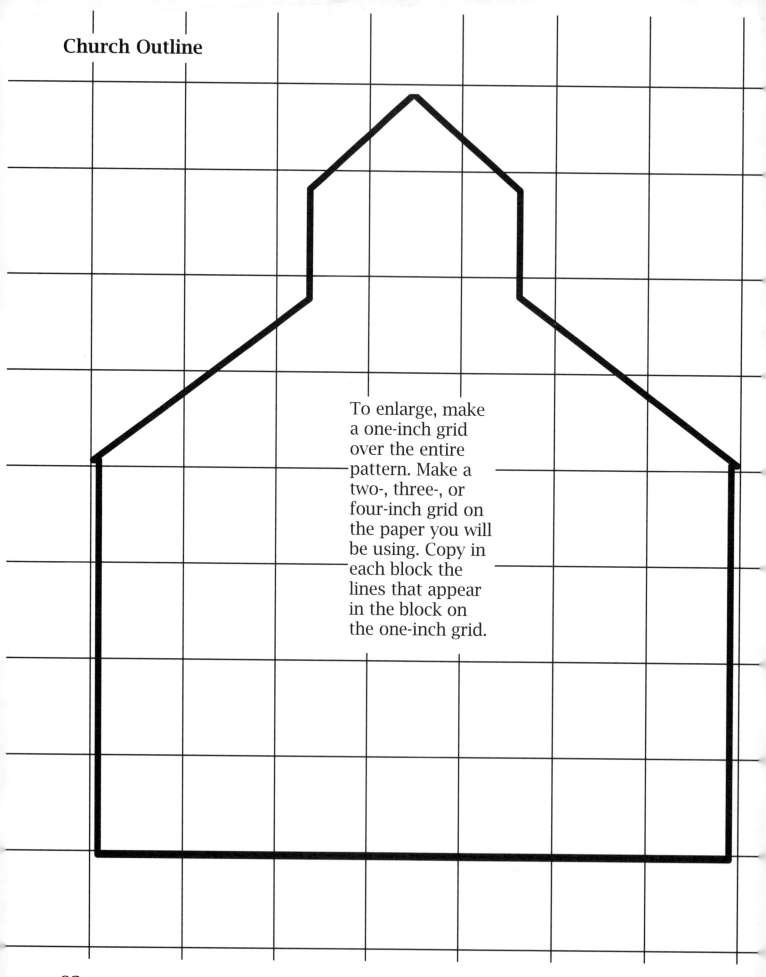

Church Outline

To enlarge, make a one-inch grid over the entire pattern. Make a two-, three-, or four-inch grid on the paper you will be using. Copy in each block the lines that appear in the block on the one-inch grid.

82

Fold paper in
half. Place
pattern so that
dotted line is
on the fold.

Take care not
to cut through
the fold.

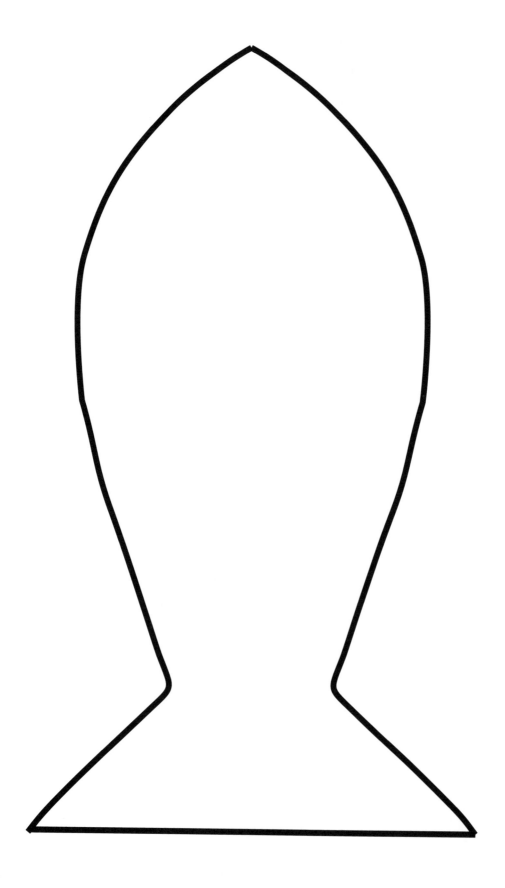

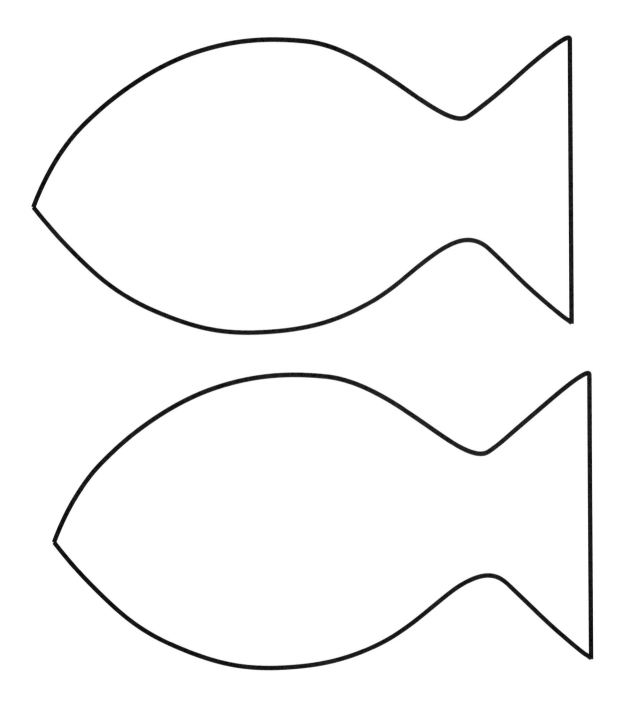

Activities by Age Groups
•••••••••••••

Older Elementary Children

Children of All Ages

Index

● ● ● ● ● ● ● ● ● ● ● ● ● ●